HELPING OURSELVES BY HELPING OTHERS

An Incarcerated Men's Survival Guide

Edited by Ben Colodzin Ph.D.
and Richard Ranta

Acknowledgments

In addition to the contributions of Vietnam veterans Edwin V. Munis and Michael "Doc" Piper—which will be discussed throughout this book—many others helped this project come together. Special thanks to Monterey County Veterans Service Officer Richard Garza and attorney/psychologist Dr. Joe Reed, whose essential assistance enabled the Correctional Training Facility (CTF) Veterans Service Office to operate; to Vietnam veterans Roland Fletcher and Phil Butler for their unwavering support of incarcerated veterans; to Correctional Training Facility Wardens Kane, Spearman, Grounds, Hattan, and Koenig, who have allowed the unit to function; to numerous prison Captains, Lieutenants and Sergeants who supported the work of the VSO, with special mention to Lieutenant Eric DaRosa for his supportive efforts; to Correctional Officer H. Romero, the current VSO direct supervisor; to Community Resource Manager Alma Tamayo for clearing various educational materials for presentation to inmates; to Juan Jose Negrete for his tireless efforts in teaching Mindfulness Meditation; to the California Veterans Benefit Fund and David De La Paz for financial and logistical support of Dr. Colodzin and the Trauma Recovery Project at CTF; to all the outside authors who graciously allowed their written articles to be reprinted here; and most essentially to all the incarcerated men who took the time to share of their experience and pass it on.

Contents

Preface

by Ben Colodzin Ph.D.

The seed impulse that led to the gathering of original writings in this book emanated from Ed Munis and Michael 'Doc' Piper. They founded the Veterans Service Office at the Correctional Training Facility (CTF) in Soledad, CA—the first inmate-run such service in the country. They helped hundreds of incarcerated veterans receive benefits they would otherwise not have received. Over the years, their reputation spread. Their information and procedures helping incarcerated veterans receive benefits they were otherwise denied circulated to more than 30 state and federal prisons. Their payback from this effort was the satisfaction they received from providing real help to those who needed it. They made the motto of their office "Helping ourselves by helping others".

Five or six years ago, Doc Piper wrote and asked me to give a lecture there about post-traumatic stress recovery. He said he had read a recovery book I wrote and was interested to develop more recovery opportunities in prison. I did that, was so impressed by what they had accomplished that I have been volunteering there for five years.

Ed died last August 2018. Doc Piper passed away this April 2019. A big loss to many who relied on their help. With the help of Richard Ranta and other veterans who have picked up the slack and continued to run the Veterans Service Office, we have invited incarcerated men who respect what Ed and Doc began to contribute their writings here. Almost all participants have been incarcerated for twenty years or more, in some cases more than 35 years. Everyone was asked to imagine what they would say—what advice they might give—if someone they cared about was recently busted and about to be sent to prison for a long term. What would you tell them? we asked.

Before they left us, Ed and Doc both wrote their own answers to this question. Ed wrote an entire booklet of useful tips for veterans, including forms needed to apply for various services.

Doc said what he wanted to say.

Answering this question is not an easy task, living with the nearly-constant threat of violence and overcrowding that is prison life these days. It requires focus, and a connection to the place in one's heart that cares, that holds compassion. Ed and Doc offered their peers a kind of compassion that worked. Over the years their efforts grew to include not only veterans but also men exposed to other life-altering traumas. Everything written here was written to show respect for the kind of compassion they practiced. The contributors have voiced their prayers and shown their caring. Thanks Ed, thanks Doc, you showed a good pathway forward.

We asked permission from prison authorities to make sure this project didn't violate their rules. We also asked that nobody write anything that violates inmate rules. There are voices of veterans, voices of former gang members, voices from many ethnicities. Each person was given the choice to make their writing signed or anonymous. There is also a recovery section which includes writings that the men in recovery groups nominated as useful for healing.

It's been an honor to get to know these men and witness first hand that prisons contain not only violence-addicted out of control people, but also many trauma survivors who have recovered their balance sufficiently to value peace and practice peacemaking in their lives. Thanks to all for showing up.

Ben Colodzin is a volunteer for the CTF Trauma Recovery Project.

Introduction

by Phil Butler, PhD, CDR, USN (ret.)

It is an honor to be asked to write the introduction to this greatly needed and useful book of information, suggestions and guidance for inmate newcomers to Soledad Correctional Training Facility (CTF).

Let me begin by saying I've had personal experience at being incarcerated, but in a different system that has some parallels to California State Prisons. I am a former Navy fighter pilot, who flew his last mission one very dark night, April 20, 1965. I went down over what then was North Vietnam. I managed to evade for 4 days and nights but was finally tracked down, captured and incarcerated in the "Hanoi Hilton" and other nearby prisons. I spent the next 2855 days & nights, 7 years and 10 months as a prisoner of war. I was released on February 12, 1973 and returned home to a wife who informed me I was being divorced and to an 8-year-old daughter who did not know me and was soon turned against me by the aforementioned wife.

My incarceration was at the hands of Vietnamese interrogators, guards and torturers. But common to all incarcerated people, I know the terrible heartache of helplessly watching the days and nights crawl by. The feeling at times that your heart is working up into your throat and eyes, like someone or something is twisting and crushing it. Yes, I know, no doubt like you, the pain of incarceration.

Unlike you, we experienced hunger, malnutrition, harassment, and even torture. The enemy Vietnamese wanted us to "confess our crimes" by writing and sometimes by making confession recordings that were played on radio broadcasts, like the infamous "Hanoi Hannah." We were isolated with no news from the outside world and very rare letters from home. Unlike you we formed covert military organizations and could rely on each other for support.

3

We found covert ways to communicate, even from solitary. Using our POW tap code, I even learned some French and German. And I taught other POW's Spanish. During my later years in bigger cells I attended many classes by fellow POW's, and learned a lot on many subjects.

That is what I call the "second life" of my autobiography "Three Lives of a Warrior" along with my other two lives, before and after incarceration as a POW. My "first life" is about growing up with an alcoholic father and abusive mother; about my military training at the Naval Academy; and about combat in Vietnam. My "third life" is about returning home and journey to recent days. I will see to it that our VSO library, currently in G Wing, will have a copy for you to read there.

Early in my POW time we came up with our motto, "Return With Honor." There were lengthy instructions that came with it but the bottom line was YOU! You knew you had to conduct yourself in such a way as to be able to look in the mirror every morning after your return, and feel proud of the guy looking back at you.

Now what about you? How do you plan on doing your time? Will you conduct yourself in such a way so as to return with honor? No doubt you don't feel very honorable about the crime that got you here. But now you have been given a second chance, as a level 1 or 2 prisoner. Will you return with honor when you get out of prison?

I've taken our POW motto for my life now, changed to "Live With Honor." That means three things for me. 1) Respect: No one is better or less than me. I will respect everyone I meet, and will also respect our planet and all life on it. 2) Commit: I will try to commit to positive things for people, issues and ideals. 3) Contribute: I will try to live my life bringing about change, making contributions that will leave people and the world a little bit better than I found them.

You might have come from a broken, addicted, or abusive family. You might have PTSD, like I did as a young man, and then after my prison experiences. So what will you do about it? Will you become an active gang member? Will you get addicted to alcohol or drugs here? Will you use your previous experiences as an excuse? Sadly, you will find plenty of opportunities to behave this way at CTF.

What will you do with your time to become a more knowledgeable and better person? Will you take all the classes and group experiences you can? Will you stay clean and sober? Will you become a role model for other inmates? Here at CTF you can choose to live with honor, to become a better man, or you can choose to go to the dark side. You can improve yourself and become a better man than the one who just got here and is reading this book.

I've been a volunteer for 5 years with our IVSO and the Vietnam Veterans groups. I had two very fine friends here: Ed Munis and Doc Piper. They made amazing contributions to hundreds of inmates in prisons all over our country, and for their families. I and many of their friends were sad that these wonderful guys passed away in prison, before they were able to experience freedom. But in my opinion, they certainly lived with honor here at CTF. And I am pleased to say that their work goes on, with IVSO representative Richard Ranta and other outside volunteer contributors.

If you are a veteran, this book has superb information for you and possibly your family. Read and follow the instructions left for you by Ed Munis and Doc Piper. In my military terms – Get off your duff and get to work on your VA applications and statements. Do something to benefit yourself and possibly your family. Also, for veterans and non-veterans alike, this book has wisdom from incarcerated guys who were here before you. They will give you a lot to think about.

OK mister. That's it. Fill out and submit your paperwork to the VA if you are a vet. Vet or not, read this book. Read all the books you can get your hands on. Volunteer for classes and groups.

No matter who you are, get to work on you. Make careful and thoughtful choices. It's your life.

No excuses. Man up. Live with Honor.

I. COMING TO PRISON

Penitentiary of the Damned

by Michael "Doc" Piper

This may seem a little dark or over the line for most of you. I know I had the same reaction when an older inmate tried to warn me of my fate. You see how well I listened to him; I am now celebrating my twenty-fourth year behind bars, because I didn't listen and thought this could never happen to me! Don't be a fool like I was!

You have been given an opportunity to get your life straight, but only if you really want to. There is nothing sadder to us older prisoners, than to see a youngster come in here with a screwed attitude, and blind to the possibilities of change for the better, knowing that they now have "All Day to Do!" Even on an installment plan, that is no way to waste your life!! You may tune all of us elders out as so much "preaching." Just trying to give you a heads-up, so LISTEN! We will be listening for a loud POP when you get your head out of your —-!

I am not inviting you to listen to every Tom, Dick, Harry, or home-boy, or to avoid any of their good advice. You need to get a serious hold of yourself and decide what your future is going to be while you still have a chance to make changes for the better. Have you figured out yet, why there are so many "Bad-ass, or Tuff guys" in prison? They are the ones that haven't got a grip on their emotions or goals in life and because of this; they want others to suffer with them for company. It took me a number of years and a trip to the hole or two, to figure this one out. It takes intestinal fortitude to tell them, "NO, I want to live my life and it isn't in here!" (LIFE on the installment plan is no life at all!)

If you haven't availed yourself of a good education, this is a good opportunity to do so. You may not be a fan of school, but I can tell you, if you ever stand a chance of getting out of here, you will be far better off with a good education behind you, and you have a perfect chance to do so.

It took me a number of years to figure things out and get my head straight. I have lived a life of assisting or helping other people, even on the outside with thirty plus years in the medical field; finally one day, by chance, I realized that "service to others is my therapy," and with the assistance of another inmate, we built and fought for, the only Veterans Service Office Service Center, in any prison in California. Again, serving others and working our way to freedom, is both mentally as well as physically rewarding. My wish for you is that it doesn't take you this long to realize you can do whatever it takes to become the person you should be, and that you deserve freedom and the values it brings! Now is the time for that life changing decision!

Right now, you need to stop and consider what got you here. If this (prison, and someone telling you what to do; when to do it; when to eat; when to sleep, etc.) is what you want the rest of your life, I will stop wasting my breath. If not, you need to become a better person. Become the person you are meant to be. Life has much more to offer than the mere existence in here, but the decision is up to you. What you do from this point on, and how you act, who you hang around and listen to, will influence the rest of your life.

Good Luck!

Michael "Doc" Piper was the Cofounder, CTF Veterans Service Office. This piece was originally written for Survival Guide 2017.

Heaven Waits — Rest in Peace Doc

by Kenneth Barnes

I've known Doc for many decades – Good Man! My name is Kenneth Barnes. Although I'm not a veteran, in honor of Doc I will submit a letter on this first term topic.

This is what I would have done with a first-time inmate. First thing I would say is to have faith and allow that to guide you to your destination. Keep your head up and always be conscious of your surroundings in a not so stressful way. Yes. You are around a lot of individuals that didn't always follow society's laws, but there are laws/rules, or what have you that one has to abide by behind these walls. For instance – if it's not yours, leave it as it lies. Try not to borrow or take attachment gifts.

Respect and stay in your lane, it will take you far. Put a plan together that will allow you to achieve success. Seek change from inside out. Try and understand and get a handle on the cause and effect that led to your incarceration. Improve connecting to your soul, where peace within develops. Treat others as you like to be treated. Stay busy educating and with various other beneficial challenges. Find like-minded people. Avoid stagnated people that will likely repeat the prison cycle. Keep a balance in your life, committing to health and staying positive.

This is my brief take on managing through an abnormal experience. Stay determined on returning to your family; other than on yourself. Family is what really matters.

Stay strong and make this your first and last trip to the big house.
God Bless.

What Would I Tell Someone Coming into Prison for The First Time?

by Byron 'Jerz' Threat

I would tell them that someone coming into prison for the first time to understand that, just because you're in prison, it doesn't define who you are from your creator, and journey throughout life. Prison can make you a better man and person, or a worse criminal. It's all about what you do with the time they gave you to do.

Doing time is not about a reunion or a party with the homies, or fellas from your hood, but it's a time to find yourself, give back, grow, and understand what your purpose in life is, or the direction you should go after your release. Take a good look at the man in the mirror and not just the haircut/shave, the pimple on one's skin, or the style of clothes, but, the person within, so you can do the knowledge of self, and grow to return back into society a different man/person than you came in as.

If you don't have an education, it's here for you. If you don't have a trade or job skills, it's here for you. If you don't have life or social skills, it's here for you. It's free and here for your betterment, so why not get it.

Time changes people and people change in time. Do your time and don't let the time do you. For the only time you waste is the time you don't use. Stay clear of debts, drugs, homosexual behavior. Don't gamble. Mind your own business. Don't owe anyone anything. Don't try to be or act tough. Have your own lane and focus on getting out and home to your family.

You don't have to be a saint or try to be a minister or a holy roller, but build a relationship with your higher power (if you believe in God). Be respectful, not a pushover. Keep it real with yourself and don't try to impress. Keep your word good, and follow the rules and regulations, plus the law of the land.

Walk with your head up and with pride, not arrogant and know that respect goes a long way, starting with yourself first. Don't get too comfortable playing, because this is not home. Be careful with who you befriend, talk with, and place in your circle, because everyone is not your friend and some will try and use you to get a step ahead or to get what they want from you.

There's strong and weak, feeble and meek, phonies, fakes, snakes, plus liars in your midst, so look and listen more than you talk. Stay observative…

Think before you talk and act. Pay attention to your environment. Keep your expectations of family/friends fair, because people will disappoint you and turn their backs on you, and sometimes, your friends become your enemy, and strangers become your family. Life is short, so make the best of each day and don't ever let anyone tell you that you can't do it or make it, because the sky is the limit if you follow your heart and keep your eyes on the prize:

YOUR FREEDOM!

(Untitled)

by Brian Park

I stepped off the bus and entered a level 4 maximum security prison at the age of 20. It was my first time in prison and thus I was filled with fear and anxiety.

I was escorted into a large housing unit where I was seated in a 'dayroom' waiting to be assigned to a cell. I watched closely as inmates roamed around the building staring at me like the new 'fish' I was.

Suddenly I heard cat calls echoing throughout the building as a transsexual inmate exited one of the showers and walked down the stairs. He (or she) had long black brittle hair, breasts bulging out under his white t-shirt, and severe acne on his cheeks. Surely he was no Victoria Secret model. The transsexual showed no emotion as the catcalls continued and I watched him walk into cell 135 as he disappeared behind a sliding steel door.

After the excitement died down, the housing unit officer began assigning cells. The officer shouted my last name and pointed to cell 135. Instead of immediately getting up and walking to my cell like the other inmates, I cemented my butt to the metal stool beneath me and began rapidly shaking my head from side to side. I told the officer he could take me to the hole, write me up, give me another life sentence, but I was not going into that cell with HIM. Thankfully, the officer understood my position, chose not to endanger my innocence, and eventually assigned me into another cell. Lesson #1: You always have a choice.

One of the choices you have to make is what ethnicity do you choose to identify as. This choice may be crucial to your personal safety, your ability to rehabilitate yourself, and can determine if you will ever be given a second chance at freedom. Whether we as inmates agree with it or not, we are sorted out through the system by race. There are 4 races distinguished in the California

Dept. of Corrections and Rehabilitation: black, white, Mexican, and 'other'. The first three races are self-explanatory; the 'other' classification requires further explanation.

'Others' usually consist of Asians, Islanders, South Americans, American Indians, and any other ethnicity that doesn't fall under black, white, or Mexican. The infamous Menendez brothers are classified as 'other' because they claim Puerto Rican ancestry of their late father.

Throughout my 24 years of incarceration, I've met 'others' who were Jewish, Russian, Brazilian, Persian, Italian, and on and on. In my opinion, choosing to be an 'other' has its major advantages. For one, 'others' are seen more like individuals-not taking part of a prison gang. If you claim to your counselors you are 'white', and then introduce yourself to all the white guys on the yard, then you are now required to follow their rules, beliefs, and commands.

If the blacks and whites riot against each other, you, as a white are required to fight, regardless of your personal opinion, circumstances, or even safety. 'Others' as a collective whole rarely ever get involved in riots, have no rules to abide by, and require no obligation to join. Perhaps the only rule is you cannot be an 'other' and any other race at the same time. There is no dual citizenship in prison.

If you want to do YOUR time, stay out of prison politics, and do not become part of a prison gang. I would suggest you carefully consider your answer to the question, "Who do you run with?"

What To Expect For Your First Time

by Everett Allen

A man got to be sharp, you got to be point blank… straight to the point (so to speak). To be honest, I was pondering on the fact, if what I offer my readers is worthy; worthy of consideration; worthy of value, and, however, it's in my deepest hopes that I tap into your understanding.

My knowledge is a peek of a man that has indulged in hate. I've been cross contaminated through the billion-dollar process of a system that creates your enemies for you and divides you, according to a race of common traits. How do I define strength" Are you capable of giving all things purpose? (It's mandatory) Can you describe when you do feel love? (It's essential)

When it's your first time stepping off that bus, with your feet and hands shackled, the first thing you consciously realize, is that life is about to make a drastic change. No more privacy. Your job pays you pennies; you wash the majority of your clothes by hand, and depression will make a strong attempt to envelop your mind. The short version on "what to do if you come to prison" will be short because my knowledge is above what your eyes can grasp at the moment; mainly for the reason that this is your first time, and I, on the other hand, have been living in this controlled world (prison) for many years.

Prison is going to be repetitious. Things are going to be routine every day. When you're in society, you're making at least thirty (30) decisions a day. In a hostile, unfriendly environment like prison, you really don't make no more than five (5) decisions a day.

For example:

1. You're going to eat chow or you're not.
2. You're going to the yard or you're not.
3. You're going to program or you're not.

For some of you, you may start your first time at a prison that has a reputation for breeding a monster inside you. My last, but not least tips for you new comers in the belly of the beast is:

1. Mind your own business.
2. Listen more than you speak.
3. Educate yourself and don't let the television raise you.
4. Work out, keep in shape.
5. Don't ever get comfortable like this is your permanent home. (Always fight the broken justice system).
6. The best associates to have are the ones that are on the same track as you're on.
7. Protect thyself at all times.

Peace...Love...Understanding
Everett Allen

Rules Upon Doing Time

by Vaughn

Incarceration: To shut in, confine!!

When I was first incarcerated, I was 17 years old, charged as an adult. At that time, they'd put you in a cell alone –single man cell. Today, you're put in population, meaning two men cell. The older homey told me about cell time. You have to know how to conduct yourself in a cell with another guy, someone you don't know. A lot of guys think that because you're in the same cell, you have to be friends with the guy you're in there with. Not true. What you have to be, is respectful to each other's space within that small confinement!!

So, the number one rule is: RESPECT… I was also told that whatever you don't have, you can do without; unless you can get it for yourself. A lot of guys get the kind of cellie that wants them to owe them, so if you drink coffee, and don't have any, they'll offer you some just so that you'll be in debt to them. Number 2) Don't take anything from a guy you don't know. If you can't get coffee, soups or anything for yourself, do without until you're able to get it for yourself! Number 3) With a cellie, you have to have a program; a cell program, i.e., what time you read, what time you write, or what time you study. A cell program helps you get alone with a cellie.

1. Be Humble and Respect People
2. Learn the Rules
3. Don't Steal or Try to Get Over on Someone
4. Be Considerate
5. Stand for Your Convictions
6. Be Open to Those That Are Looking Out for You and Are Not Trying to Use You

Following Rules

by Anonymous

Rules are a big thing in prison. You break some of those rules and you could end up getting hurt or even killed. Things in prison are much different than on the streets. People that were against each other on the streets might be on the same side in prison. It takes some time to get used to being in prison. You might have friends, homeys, and such in prison with you, but if you do something that's not accepted in prison, they might be the ones who have to make sure that you understand that you did wrong. That could be by: being talked to, being beat up, being stuck with a knife, being slashed with a razor, or even killed.

Sometimes a person doesn't get the true meaning of what you say. Because they are from a different area, group, gang, or a different race, things can be misconstrued and they think you're saying one thing, when you're really saying something different. Everyone interprets words in different ways. They depend on your experiences growing up, what you saw, what you went through personally, what your beliefs are, or what you've been taught. Life is different for all of us. It's essential that you make sure that what you say is what the other person is hearing. One word or one inflection of your voice the wrong direction, can trigger another person to be angry, lash out, lose their cool, be disrespected, or cause you great bodily harm. It's something that most people in prison learn to do and to do it with respect. Respect is a key lifeline in prison.

Respect is how prisoners live. If you're disrespected, most prisoners will get angry fast and may lead to an escalation of that anger, which could result in you fighting that person.

Each institution has certain areas for each group of prisoners. Each group has an area on the yard, in the wing/dorm you live in, in the chow hall, in the gym, in the church, and even in certain self-help groups. If you go into another area without permission, things can get out of hand for you. By staying to your own group's area, you avoid any consequences coming your way.

Most of the rules in prison are not hard to follow. Just keep your eyes and ears open to what is going on around you. Follow what the older prisoners tell you and you should be okay. The older prisoners have been around and know how to school the younger ones. These days, this doesn't happen. This causes problems within the younger inmates. They don't know the rules and act like they do on the streets. They don't understand respect as it is in prison. If they are schooled, they can understand what is expected of them and others. If not, chaos ensues and usually results in one or more inmates being physically assaulted or worse; a melee or a riot.

Rules have their advantages as well as respect does. They can make your time in prison a much less strenuous time. Take the time to seek out information regarding the proper etiquette of prison life. This will help while you seek self-help programs, schooling, or vocational programs.

It's all up to you how you want to do your time!

My Younger Self

by Anonymous

Gotta ask the question first:

Do you know the difference between a Lie and a Fairy Tale?

A Fairy Tale always starts out: Once Upon A Time…

A Lie starts out: Check this out…

I ask that question simply because of all the stories that people tell, or when they want to 'give advice,' when in fact, the advice is the worst that one could take. Many times, I had heard a story told and it always started with Check this out…, and one should as a matter of course, weigh the stated facts upon the legitimacy of the storyteller.

The belief that coming to prison holds a certain expectation that one must follow and if they do not, they will eventually pay the consequences: the politics of prison life. This most certainly is an outdated paradigm, meaning that it is just not the standard anymore.

It was once the obligation of the older convict to set the example, so that the 'new fish' or youngster was set upon the right path. The older convict is supposed to take the younger one 'under the wing' and ensure that he is 'schooled' and does not break or violate any of the prison code. Today, this in fact is the worst thing that can happen. It is one thing to be 'schooled' by an older homeboy; it is quite another thing to be used.

My advice to a younger self, when you don't know what you should do when you lack the knowledge of what the community values are of your race, watch those around you.

It will most certainly come to you when you see the degradation that ensues. Don't get yourself mixed up with the 'Too hard for the yard' guy, who does nothing but 'talk up' his time in prison, uses narcotics for addiction purposes, gives his commissary to feed a habit, then mooches in the same ten minutes space, after going to store and paying off the connection.

I would hope that a right-minded individual will notice how you stay away from such people and will provide you with a pathway to getting yourself an education. Perhaps, even helping open up opportunities to gain vocational training; help improving your work skills; fostering your artistic abilities; or some other time-consuming project that will keep you away from those that are toxic to your return to society.

And by no means does this mean that you should be afraid to seek help from those who can provide it, but provide it without the expectation of some financial gain or other favor that can cause you to sink to their level.

There will be times when you will become uneasy, by the politics of the yard, but hold fast, keep a clear head, protect yourself from the harm that others will set upon you, and keep to your morals. If you can do this, then there is hope that you will help keep you from returning to prison. Those people, the 'Too hard for the yard, level 10 killers,' the drug addicts that 'talk up' their prison history and corresponding events, the 'homeboy,' none of them will ever have your best interest at heart. They will only try to use you for their benefit, even when they seem to be the best dudes you have ever met. I can guarantee that when the shit hits the fan, they will not be by your side in the hole; providing you with any monetary compensation for your actions that they direct; no, they simply will be gone, looking for their next victim.

Be your own man!

Prison Rules to Live By

by Rickey Allen Sonney-
Convict, California Penal System, 35 Years Total Incarceration

- Don't drink (alcohol), do drugs; gamble or fuck queers unless you pay for it up-front. In other words, no CREDIT EVER. Pay for everything up-front.
- Always keep your word, no matter what, period! You say something; then do it- NO EXCEPTIONS.
- Learn boundaries; yours and others.
- Learn to say "NO." The hardest part of saying no is the first minute.
- Nothing is free in prison. NOTHING. If you think it's free, it's not worth having and in the long run, you really won't appreciate it is as if you had worked/paid for it yourself.
- Strings are always attached to FREE.
- There are only two kinds of money in prison; yours and everyone else's.
- Only three kinds of business in prison; YOURS, OTHERS, and GOD'S. Stay in your own business.
- Q.T.I.P. Quit taking it personal.
- When you try to understand another convict, know his potential for being both a friend and an enemy.
- Learn to be comfortable being uncomfortable.
- Get an education, it's fucking FREE! Don't be a dumb-ass.
- Don't be an "ASSHOLE!"
- Just be you, not what others want you to be.
- Upgrade vocationally.

- Get self-help, you need it; you're living with another man in a bathroom.

- Commit to non-violence.

- Possess integrity.

- Have respect for your fellow prisoner (some of them are potentially dangerous).

- Everyone has bad days, so will you.

- Don't borrow other people's possessions.

- Read and write.

- Reconcile with everyone you have done wrong.

- Ask why.

- Get spiritual (There's plenty to choose from, check out different religions).

- Exercise. No matter your age.

- Maintain your health at all cost (never be too proud to see the doctor, dentist, psychologist).

- Don't live with a home-boy (you'll thank me later).

- Please shower.

- Maintain your personal hygiene.

- Keep your cell clean.

- Find a good celly (they're hard to find, you might have to compromise).

- You always have a choice. There are "NO" neutral choices, "NONE." They all have consequences.

- Have humility. Always admit when you're wrong.

- Don't ask the meaning of life. Answer the questions life is asking you.

- It's never too late to do the right thing. You don't have the rest of your life; just what's left of it.

- No one is guaranteed tomorrow.

- Anger is your most valuable possession. "Don't Lose It!"

- If you hate another man, you are his slave.

- Just do your time.

- Know the difference between an inmate and a convict. (I can't teach you this.)

- Never give prisoners any information not directly asked for. Keep your privacy.

- Never underestimate anyone.

- Never think you can't be worked. There's always someone slicker than you.

- Listen and watch twice as much as you speak.

- No whining or complaining while in prison, suck it up.

- If you don't like something, remember these four words; "DON'T COME TO PRISON."

- If you don't like it or wouldn't want it to happen, then, don't do it to others. # 1 Life Lesson!

(Untitled)

by Bruce Walker

"As I look back, I would tell anyone first coming to prison this: Since you will most likely owe restitution for criminal damages, you should know that CDCR can take 55% of any money that will be put onto your books in prison, and apply that towards restitution. If you have any money, it is a good idea if you can load up your money on your books while in county, before coming to prison. Once that money is on your books in county, it can transfer with you to CDCR without them taking any for restitution or taxing you. I hope this can help some people balance out their need to pay restitution with their own basic survival needs.

Things I Would Tell A Newcomer To Prison

by Anonymous

THINGS YOU SHOULD DO

1. If you didn't have a high school diploma or a G.E.D., you should sign up for education, so you can get one, either one.
2. Sign up for one of the many self-help groups.
3. Once you are placed in a cell, ask your cell mate about the different areas on the yard, where the phones and canteens are located, etc.
4. Find out what religious services are available. They offer many, whatever faith you are.

THINGS YOU SHOULD NOT DO

1. Don't just walk up to someone or to a group, without first getting to know them and what they are all about.
2. Do not gamble, period!
3. Do not borrow money or canteen items if you cannot pay it back, it is best not to borrow anything from anyone at any time.
4. If you are not in a gang, don't join one.
5. Don't act like you know everything. If you don't know something it is best to ask someone, instead of playing it off like you do. That could end up getting you into trouble.

How Do I Get My Package or Appliances?

by Anonymous

For those of you that are coming to prison for the first time, I can only give you the information that I have or that I have experienced. If you want to get a quarterly package or any appliance (such as: TV, radio, tablet, CD's, etc.), you will need to find a catalog from one of the companies that CDCR has approved. Ask your cellie how to get your quarterly package and appliances. Most of the time, they have been here for some time, and they know the process and how it works. When I first came to prison, I was schooled (taught the do's and don'ts, by an inmate who had been down (in prison) for a while. Most prisons still work that same way, but you will find that some don't.

There are a few choices and you might want to check out the prices before you send off the first order form you get. Prices vary as far as the companies do. Some have decent prices and some are overpriced. Be a well-informed shopper before you buy. Check out the return policies. Check out how to get the appliance fixed or replaced, if it comes damaged. Pay attention to those details and you should be okay.

Most prisons, you will have to go to a Package Room (R & R, here at CTF), to pick up your quarterly package or your appliances. Some prisons might have the Package room right on the yard. Some will issue passes with a specific time to come and pick up your stuff. Make sure that you do what is required of you in order to receive your package or appliance in a timely manner.

If you don't, some C/O's will hold onto your things for a certain period of time, before they allow you to get them. In other words, DON'T PISS OFF THE C/O's! They have control of who gets what and when they can get it. Follow their rules, as you should do anyway, if you want to get yourself out of prison.

You can also ask a member of the Inmate Advisory Committee, which you should have a representative in your wing, block, dorm, who will have all the information you will need, and should have catalogs for all the companies. Make sure that you take the time to make a good decision. You don't want to be an unhappy buyer, once you receive your package. If dissatisfied, you can also write to the company and let them know what you are not satisfied with. Most times, if you do, they will respond and try to make it right with you. They don't want to lose a paying customer. I have had to do this, and the response was good. They sent what was not in the order, free of charge to me. These companies like repeat customers and they will usually do everything they can to keep you as their customer.

I think I covered everything I could for you. Make sure you seek out all the information you can and make an informed decision!

Prison Life: The Book

by Anonymous

It all starts when you leave the county jail and get on the bus; that is when your life changes FOREVER. You are no longer the grandfather, uncle, brother, father, cousin, nephew, son, friend, husband, etc.… That's who you used to be. You become an INMATE, out of sight, out of mind. The people you thought would be there for and have your back are the ones that leave you first! And people that you didn't expect to be there? There are some that do support you and have your back. This is when you truly see who loves and cares about you the most.

Now, let's talk about prison. When you first get to prison, they place you in reception, you can be there up to six months; this is where you start, learning how to 'do time'. If you are a first timer, they try to place you in a cell with someone from the area you live in, or from a gang from that area. Then they label you by who you hang around, so you have to let them know right off the bat that you're not a part of that, or they will say you're from a gang, or you hang out with them.

Then they put you in a cell with another person, and most of the time they can teach you how to 'do time', because it's certain ways you do things. Because the cells are so small, first thing is to respect each other's space, and things. Try not to lie on the floor at the same time. If you use the restroom, put a sheet up for privacy. And, 'drop one, flush one' is the rule, always clean up behind yourself. Wash your clothes and shower or birdbath, roll your bed up, get up in the morning before the doors open for chow, and be ready for WHATEVER because you never know what's going to happen. Always pay attention and be alert at all times.

If you don't have something, don't borrow anything from nobody, because they will want something in return. Don't gamble, don't steal, don't mess around with the homosexual, and stay away from the gangs. Because once you get labeled as a gang member, people only know you as that, and now if you have committed yourself to them, you lose your identity. You forget who you are and you become what they tell you you are. You stop caring about everything and everybody, this place makes your heart hard. You become bitter and you stop caring. You lose focus on the things that are important. It seems like you lose everything: your wife, kids, job, house, car, family, etc. – people stop accepting your collect calls, and all you have then is this place, or your faith in your higher power, whatever that may be.

Some people turn to drugs and alcohol to cope with this being locked up. You no longer have control of your life. You now belong to CDCR, they own you. They control your whole life. They tell you when to eat, sleep, talk, shower, use the restroom, when you can go outside and when to go in, where you can and can't go and do! They want to know where you're at, 365 days a year, 24 hours a day, 7 days a week. So you have to be a strong-minded person, or it's going to break you down, and you will be worse off than before you came.

So the best thing to do is to stay out of trouble, because if you're looking for it, it is easy to find.

There's always somebody willing to help you fuck up your life even more than what it already is.

But you don't need that, or you wouldn't be reading this.

Another way is to mind your own business, keep your mouth shut and your eyes open; get your own stuff. Learn as much as you can, go back to school or take a trade, go to self-help groups. Choose positive people to be around, that want the same things you want. Stay in contact with your family and friends and kids. Use this time productively to become a better person and get to know yourself.

Follow the rules - the 'do's and don'ts'. ALWAYS and I do mean ALWAYS show respect to others. Be careful who you become friends with, make sure you get to know them first, watch out for the con artists, the scammers and the scam-less, because they will try to use you or befriend you, or set you up for failure. They act like they care, but will throw you to the wolves the first chance they get, don't tell them your personal business or introduce them to your family, because if they can't talk to their family, there's probably a good reason, like they burned their bridges there, and that's not the type of people you want to be around. I always say, if you can't invite them to dinner at your house, then maybe you shouldn't be around them yourself. Right?

Think about it.

The first three days you move in with a new cellie, make sure that you're compatible, and if you're not, get out of there right away! That way you don't get caught up with their bullshit, so if you're not on the same page-like. Trying to better yourself and go home-then don't put yourself in that position. Because all that LOOKS good to you may not be good for you.

Smile now, cry later? Because at some point there's a price that comes with it, because

NOTHING IN PRISON IS FREE. They may say it is, but somewhere down the line they're going to want a favor from you. And when you can't do it, all hell is going to break loose. But hopefully, you never have to experience none of this hands-on, because THIS PRISON LIFE IS NO JOKE.

I wouldn't wish this on anybody. This is pure hell. All the negativity around you, all day, every day! And all it takes is you to fall weak to what is going on around you, and it's a rap. One thing can take all the years you've been working on yourself and throw it all away in a split second. So you have to decide what's important to you-changing your life, or proving a point? Don't let your PRIDE be your downfall, be your own MAN, make your own DECISIONS, because at the end of the end, you have to do this time. One way or the other, you can do it easy or you can do it hard. Because they got something for you (laugh) they will make you mind somebody, one way or the other, or you can stay here for the rest of your life.

That's up to you. Only you know how you want to live your life, or waste it. Shit, you will wake up one day. I just hope it's not too late or you're too old or both.

So if you're reading this (please) don't take these words I'm telling you for granted. Because I'm 'seasoned by grief' and QUALIFIED by EXPERIENCE. Trust me, been there, done that! I always say, if I can change, then anybody can. And that's real. It shouldn't have had to come to me taking a man's life, for me to realize how SERIOUS THIS IS. To lose my wife, kids, home, business, cars, everything. Family members have passed-my mom, dad, aunties, uncles, cousin, friends-and I couldn't even go to the funeral. Tell me that's not enough, them I don't know what is.

So after reading this, do the right thing, seek help, and put in the work! Good luck and God

Bless.

Your friend, (name withheld)

My Beloved Brother

by Curtis Smith

Now that you've been sentenced to prison, here are some of the do's and don'ts that will keep you alive and thriving in a place that even your wildest imagination would have never placed you in. Know first, that you must come back home alive, versus in a coffin. Therefore, you must know that prison is not the beginning of the end. You will be afforded many opportunities to better yourself, if you choose. There are many trades to be learned, multiple self-help groups to improve your character, and even opportunities to attend colleges that you may obtain a degree.

Just like in your old life prior to you becoming incarcerated, you'll be faced with the choice to either do good or evil. I can only hope that your days of evil have ended.

You'll have more time on your hands than you've ever had in your life. That's why they call prison "doing time." In the beginning your mind will be all over the place as you ponder how the heck you ended up in such a dark place. I can't tell you how to make these thoughts go away, but I can tell you how to not allow them not to overwhelm you, as your emotions will be taking you on a daily rollercoaster ride.

You must find something to preoccupy your time, whether it is reading, writing loved ones, poetry, a book, exercising, or playing sports. You need to stay active. It is truly a must. If you believe in God, you need to draw upon asking for His direction and assistance. Instead of having a continual pity party, you need to make yourself available to the people who are less fortunate than you. You'll know them when you see them. One of the greatest things you can do for the healing process to get started, is to make yourself available to the people around you. Without being a "mark," help people whenever reasonably possible, and do not let the color of a person's skin deter you in your efforts. Keep your eyes open, being drawn to the things that are good, and being repelled, by the things that are not. Don't smoke, drink, do drugs, or anything to harm your body; remembering your objective is to return home alive, a better person than the one that separated you from the family and the things you love.

Write your family continually, even if they don't write back. You have far more time on your hands than they do, and besides, no one writes letters anymore. Just like you are in shock being a new arrival, they too, are in shock dealing with your absence. So, please don't burden them with your selfish expectations to write you or be at your beckoning call. You left them, not they you.

One last thing, don't bind your family and loved ones up in your selfish expectations. Use this time to get to know yourself, reflect on your past life and see where you made wrong turns, review the situation that landed you in prison, from an alternative perspective, one that would not have taken away your freedom, and practice those ways. Be a giver and not a taker. Whatever relationship you had with people prior to your incarceration, don't allow guilt or shame to erode it. If you value the relationship, then work to keep it. Don't be afraid to say I'm sorry, or ask for forgiveness. Both will help you heal.

If you are a person of faith, draw upon it and use this time as an opportunity to form the most intimate relationship with the Creator as humanly possible. Amen.

II. BEING IN PRISON

Get On with It

by Anonymous First Termer

Well, if you are a lifer, stop feeling sorry or mad. Get over it and start working on your freedom. Believe me, you have a chance to go home, but you have to put in the time and work at it, by going to groups, learning about your crime, why you lived the way you did, learning new traits, getting a G.E.D., college degree, and a key part of all this is participate. Don't bullshit yourself. If you have a family, keep them in mind. Don't do drugs, if you never have, don't try to be like the other guys.

Respect is earned by your ways, not by violence. That's called fear. Mind your own business and keep your opinions to yourself. If not, you will get in trouble. Do not be a follower, be you.

Don't brag or lie.

Common sense is not too common. Use yours, be careful with who you hang with. I say this only if you want to go home. I'm paying for my choices in my action, because, when you go to the Board, all your actions will be judged. So I hope you do better than I have.

One other thing, don't drop the soap in the shower! Just joking. But no horse playing.

Prison Survival Guide

by Oscar Gutierrez

My best advice to someone who is just coming in to the prison system (CDCR), is to always be respectful to everybody, inmates and staff. Some individuals might not give them the same respect and treatment you give them, but at least you did your part as a decent human being. Try to get familiar with the staff you deal with on a regular basis, as one day, you might need something from them. Also, be courteous, like some of our parents taught us. Say "Thank you" and "please," when appropriate. That goes a long way. Also important, be mindful and aware of your actions and surroundings. This could help you avoid breaking CDCR rules, as well as "inmate's rules." This could help you avoid something in general.

If you're not sure about something, ask somebody. When you get to a new place (prison), you should be asking plenty of questions anyways. Where do I sit down to eat? Where do I exercise, or use the phone, etc.…? Again, you're just trying to avoid problems. In prison, there are plenty of boundaries and "out of bounds" areas that one needs to be mindful of. Some are CDCR designated boundaries and some are inmate-made.

Furthermore, be clean and take care of your personal hygiene. Nobody wants to be around a "dirt-bag!" Try as best you can, to look good and "presentable." Remember, look good and feel good! Also, develop a daily routine that will make you feel decent and productive, when you lay it down at the end of the day. A productive daily program should consist of a decent job/work assignment, regular exercise, educational and self-help groups, and regular church attendance. This will help your time fly and at the same time, it will keep you away from the negative aspects of prison that will get you "caught up" in unnecessary situations that will keep you in prison longer than you need to.

With all these in mind aim to improve yourself. You're in prison for a reason. Try to distance yourself from those character defects that got you in prison in the first place. We all have a true self, with plenty of goodwill. Find your true self! The goal is to walk out of prison a better man/woman than when you came in. Always keep in mind the people that care about you the most – family and loved ones.

Become a Better Human Being for Yourself

by Kirivudy Soy

It's your first time in prison and you're going to deal with a lot of personalities. I personally observe people, to see if they are aggressive, before interacting with them; from a simple chess game, to volleyball. There are sore losers and good sports. It's good to talk to your celly to find out boundaries. My advice; know your boundaries! It's time to change and find the roots why you are in prison. Take self-help groups, like: 12-step programs, like A.A., C.G.A. (Criminal and Gang Members Anonymous), to combat your destructive behaviors. Drugs and Alcohol may have contributed to your crime and incarceration. Fast money is an addiction.

So, apply the tools you learn in self-help groups. Pray to God, if you have a bad celly; have patience, and find a new one. Go to church and hang out with positive people, unless you want to be in and out of prison for the rest of your life. I've met people doing short times, coming in and out for a total of 15 years, but at different times. It may have been 5 – 15 terms.

Some people enjoy prison and don't care. You will see people that are stubborn; that are old and grouchy, doing endless time. Ask yourself, "Will I be him or will I be free? Should I continue my lifestyle or change?" Don't use violence. Be assertive. Use "please", "thank you", and "excuse me".

It's hard time if you make it hard. Take college classes while it's free and learn a trade or vocation. You will get time off your sentence and go to the parole board earlier if you are a lifer or go home earlier if you don't have a life sentence.

Don't give up hope if you're a lifer. I've seen so many lifers go home. Laws are changing. TV is a waste of your time, so enjoy it at night or on weekends only. Learn a second language and write a daily schedule. Time will go by fast when you are programming with positive people.

Less stress and problems. Let go of your old beliefs. Illegal activity in prison will get you into trouble, inmates will tell on you, so behave and don't get write-ups.

Become a better human being for yourself, God, family, and your children, if you have some. They love you and please love yourself. Pray and forgive yourself because Jesus will.

A Note to My Younger Self

by Frank Hand

When I first came to prison, I knew nothing, but I have learned a whole lot in my 34 years being incarcerated. First, never borrow anything. If you borrow something, like a jar of coffee, it doesn't matter how much if costs; if you don't pay your debts, someone will feel disrespected. There are men in prison that will kill you over one dollar ($1.00). In prison, your word is your bond. If your word is no good, you're no good. Never loan anything to anyone, even your friend. If they don't pay it back, what will you do about it, write it off and look weak? If other prisoners find out about it, they will either; try and talk you into doing something about it, or decide that you're easy prey.

My uncle, Johnny Ray, was a biker. He told me to walk slowly because there is no place to go and hide. He also said to drink lots of water, because every other liquid costs money. Do your own time!

If you're already a gang member, then that is who you will be in prison. Once you say yes, you can never say no! And if you think that joining a gang will make you safe, you will still answer to them. Walking alone is your choice, but you must live or die, by the choices you make. I joined the United States Army and swore allegiance to them and the United States Constitution to them, against all enemies.

We all must answer to someone and we are being watched at all times. It might be God, the State, big brother, so think long and hard before you act. Respect others and they will, most times, respect you.

A Word of Advice for First Termers

by Leroy S. Wilson

First, you start forgiving yourself if you want to change your life. Then, get in touch with your higher power and ask for His or Her forgiveness. That's the start if you want it. Let your days of violence end now. Start working on yourself right out of the gate. If you have to go before the Parole Board in 12 years, etc....it would be of your best interest to start now.

Violence has been lauded as the supreme solution and consistently been excused as acceptable behavior for human beings. If you want to continue in this manner, or breaking the laws of the prison system, you will get caught. Most of them do. This is not a place where you break laws, if you want to change, you will learn eventually how not to break rules, but to respect them. Do your best on living a disciplinary free life style- "no write ups." Don't let any man or group of men dictate your further freedom.

You have a lot of work ahead of you. Maybe start off with learning a trade. I hope you have a high school diploma. If not, work hard to earn yours. Don't overwhelm yourself mentally if you have a higher power you believe in, for example, God. The chapels here at Soledad have programs to keep you out of the way. You'll be able to build positive relationships.

If you're a lifer, you're going to have to dig into your life to figure out how you got to this point.

Start early if you wish. Believe me, it will help you share in groups like: AA, for instance.

To get to courage, you'll go through fears. Sitting in groups, staying silent, because of fear; it can take years to overcome this fear. A jump-start is getting involved in an "Insight Program," at Sister Mary Hodges or PREP at the address below, or you can read your bulletin board in the wing for more information about what programs PREP offers. Write to:

> PREP
> P.O. Box 77850
> Los Angeles, CA 90007

and ask for the insight program.

If you're athletic enough, get into playing sports, but if you still have anger issues, prison basketball might not be for you. Carry yourself with confidence, son. You know why I call you son? It's because you're worth it!

Stay safe!

(Untitled)

by F. Mendoza

I used to think that life was a bunch of meaningless random events with no purpose. I was twenty-one years old when I came to prison for the first time. I ended up doing ten years on a six to life sentence. I had served my country in the U.S.M.C. and really believed that my military record would have kept me from going to prison. I came to prison with a very bitter attitude towards the Justice system and began to use heroin and whatever drug I could get my hands on to get high, and I really thought I was actually getting rid of the pain and the hurt. But what I didn't realize was that I did myself more harm than fix anything.

The day came that I paroled, but I did so with not really knowing that I was hooked on heroin. I continued to use and was always making excuses that I could quit whenever I wanted to! I have spent my entire life locked up in prison, due to my addiction to drugs and very poor choices in life. That in itself should have woke me up to the waste of life that I've given to the Department of Corrections. Oh, sure, we blame everything and others for all the wrongs and bad things that happen to us, but the reality of it remains. No one is to blame except ourselves, and the sooner you or I can except that as fact and admit to ourselves that our lives are very unmanageable and powerless, and get right with society, that's when our life will begin to change for the better. You have to really dig deep down inside yourself and seriously go through your whole life timeline, to find out why you turned out the way you did. Then, ask yourself, "Is this what I really want out of life?" Believe me, crime and prison only make things worse. So, my advice to younger men is to stay in school and learn all the knowledge you can. Yeah. Life is not easy, but if you work hard at what you want to be, all doors are open in being a successful, responsible person in this life. If you really, really, think about it, life is not that hard, if you live by the rules of society.

Sam's Advice and Memories

by Sam Dubyak

As most people find out, through trial and error, and OBSERVING; the yards are very territorial as to race, gang affiliations, and often just culture. I stopped to tie a shoelace. There was this empty table and benches. Not knowing, I sat down to tie that shoelace, when a small group of inmates approached me and asked, "Are you a Crip?" Not quite understanding the question, I simply said, "What?" They said, "You must be a Crip, because you're sitting at a Crip table." I said, "Do I look like a fucking Crip?" I finished tying my shoelace and left.

Moral of the incident is to observe the area and the people.

Don't simply walk through another "groups" area. Walk around their space. You do not need to come across as scared, but just being "prison respectful," as prison respect is all that some inmates have or know. It's part of prison life. The worst thing you will probably hear coming from an inmate is, "I'm going to get my respect." These people are referred to as "state raised" inmates. They've been in prison basically since childhood and never learned to earn respect, but think respect comes from intimidating another individual, or by force. It's best to stay away from these mental issues.

NEVER loan any form of electronics, not even a watch or batteries to anyone, unless you never expect to get them back in the same condition. When they steal/switch batteries for their own equipment, thinking that everyone is as stupid or gullible as they are, you are the one that lost items.

Never loan anything to anyone, because it's gone forever. Your moral code or integrity will not be returned to you as you would do to someone else. It just doesn't work that way. Develop a few trusted friends to pal around with, to share a soda or other items, as long as the other persons are reciprocating the gesture. Don't share a can of soda with another inmate's mouth. So many inmates have disease that you don't want to even know about. Then, you go on a visit to see your family and pass it along to your wife or children; if you've ever been lucky enough to have a family. Don't take bites of food from another man's food. It's not being paranoid, it's just being considerate of your own family and COMMON SENSE.

As in the deep blue ocean, shit seeks its own level and that can be said for the yard also. Observe the first few days, a new or commonly called "fish" can find his own, 'bus' (group from the same gang/neighborhood) and whatever drugs are available. NEVER get into debt buying drugs, as I have seen and been next to people getting stabbed and killed over drug debts. Drug debts only cause you to abuse your family and children by taking food and their needs from them to pay off your debts. That's a sorry person in my view that deprives their family because of their own issues.

Never buy from people selling cookies, candy, sodas, etc., on a 2 for 1 price. If you need some cookies that bad, get some self-control and do without until you can buy from the canteen.

Don't make calls on the phone for other inmates, unless you have really developed a trusting friendship over time. You don't want another sleaze-bag having your family's information, so they can abuse them financially in any way.

Don't let your cell mate, assuming you're in a 2-man cell; talk you into letting his 'friend' come into the cell while you are on the yard. Remember, any drugs or contraband in your cell becomes yours when it's found, plus, if your cell mate is stupid enough to want to have another person in the cell while you are gone, it's usually to share drugs. Dogs have noses, and it comes out when staff search.

Try to use your time in a worthwhile or meaningful way; education, GED, college courses are often free or at a minimum cost. Someday you will go home and if you became 'state raised,' all you can say around family or at a job interview is, "bro, dog, bonaroo, that's slamming, etc.). It's not fair to judge people at an interview, but that is what an interview is for in the first place.

THINK before you get all the state raised tattoos on your face and neck. There's nothing wrong with tattoos, if that is your thing, but you will one day be around normal people, and how you present yourself and look is what your character will also be judged on.

Show honest respect to both staff and inmates, and expect the same in return. If you are not getting it back, then move on to someone else. No matter what you may think or feel, there are assholes on both sides of the fence. You don't have to be the asshole first.

Don't let anyone bully you or intimidate you, as the majority of 'state raised' have no idea what manners are.

Don't butt into private conversations. Once again, observe as you walk up to friends. Simply ask,

"Private conversation," and they will say no and invite you to sit down. Also, never walk up to an empty space at a table and simply sit down. ASK! Its simple manners and maybe you just make a new friend. Not all inmates are bad, mean, or state raised scum bags living their lives where they belong. There are good people that made a mistake or error in judgment.

If you have available, make use of any military or Veterans' groups. If you have ever served our country, there are good people in those groups and sometimes, as in my personal case, I made better friends in those groups than I ever had in the free world.

Keep your mind active education wise, even if it's the television, with game shows such as

Jeopardy, to think a little. Don't get hung up all day long on dominos or cards, as one day you will wake up and years have gone and your mind is still at the same mental level. It is a recognized fact that a person's maturity does not advance while incarcerated. An old saying we used was, "He's 35 going on 15," figure it out yourself.

Don't become a pack rat in your cell, neatness shows that you care about yourself. Take care of your health as best as you can; walk, run, exercise. I would walk for hours with a friend and we often never said a word; thinking time. Write family, but don't burn bridges behind you if you don't know what that phrase means, well, it's basically don't shit on anyone who someday may be able to help you.

Stay safe and well. Be aware of your surroundings, but don't get paranoid. Life is too short.

For the Survival Guide

by Hector Arriaga

To the new men who are struggling to get by with so many changes and much to learn. As we all do by trial and error. Listen, watch, pay close attention and learn to ask before speaking or taking action, legal or illegal. Keeping your nose clean (mind your own business)—respect is an action given, not taken. It's not just a word that we deserve or need to earn and gain. You learn more by making yourself available for a minute of your time to those who have a minute to listen, and vice-versa—because we live in this world of needs, wants, and desires. You may find yourself with people that really want to share as well as those who really want to listen, and find that what works for them might not work for you.

Also, rumors-be very wise to know the main source. Did you see it or read it? Where? From whom did you hear about it? Let's see it in print.

Stay busy with the programs available, maybe not because you need them (short time), but because you learn more from those who are sharing. Don't be afraid to ask even if it seems stupid to ask such a question. But most and best of all, share—even if it's Kibbles and Bits— don't give up. Just keep chipping at it so you'll find that it wasn't such a big deal after all. I'm saying this because of my shame and bashfulness my entire life due to my upbringing early in life. So don't sell yourself short or think otherwise of yourself because other people see it as weakness and love and thrive on it. It is very important to know—who were you? What happened? And WHO YOU ARE NOW.

Let's suppose you see yourself as a property investment. You are the property. Your payments are your investments. What payments can you make? Physical activity. Education—school, groups, and programs. Self-help. The equity you get back is a growth in confidence, believing more in yourself.

And you learn from the moral principles of other people. The value? You are more valuable to yourself, family, and others. Credibility? They believe in you. Trust, rely and depend on you. You become an asset, not a liability.

In the storm of struggles during incarceration, it may seem pointless to care about positive changes you make, but tell me, what is a better way to do time than time doing you? When facing trouble or trouble facing you, ask yourself this same question: Do I really need this? because violence breeds and generates more and more violence, an endless cycle of violence.

Ask yourself not because you're scared and afraid, because a grown mature man has more sense and vitality to seek a solution and not the problem, because definitely there is a solution. Just give yourself a minute to defuse or make amends for something that was overlooked.

There is little to no time after the unlock, to get to where you're going. That is beyond our control and it always seems to get worse the more you pay attention to it. Some things we have to learn to live with and adjust, but always be ready to be quick to listen when spoken to, slow to speak and quick to forgive, even if it wasn't your fault. Because sometimes we ourselves are going through the motions of something, just as they would. And it is very important when you refer or talk to someone by name or alias whichever they may prefer, you'll find it much easier to get their attention properly if you ask first. Don't demand. There is a big difference. You'll see in their reaction. "Do unto others as you would have them do unto you."

Worthy of their Sacrifices

by Shon

By 2018, I had already been incarcerated for nearly seven years. I had coasted through the system, took classes just for show and tried to avoid the everyday drama of the prison yard politics. I continued to blame my victim – my wife, Renee – for the crime I am responsible for; I took no accountability and I just didn't "get it." I wanted to falsely fill the voids to my life and get out of prison as soon as possible.

A Life Changed

On 17 Feb 18, I was called to the property room and my life was forever changed that day. I hadn't ordered any items and I really didn't want to depart my weekend TV shows, but, reluctantly, I got dressed and went to the property room where I had to wait in a line outside, during a Midwest winter. I made it to the window, signed the yellow property receipt and received a book with some papers attached. The book, titled *Stories of Faith and Courage from the War in Iraq and Afghanistan*, looked cool with the face of a soldier on the cover. I read the heartfelt letter of support that was filled with compassion, knowledge and direction from Gold Star Mom Debbie Lee. Her son, Marc Lee, was the first Navy SEAL killed in Iraq (2 Aug 06, in the Battle for Ramadi). I remembered Marc's death as I was attending combat medic school that year.

I turned the pages and saw a handwritten message on the dedication page. I studied those monumental words, written in red ink, and it felt like a prize-fighter had punched me in my solar plexus.

My breathing paused. I felt my pulse pounding, my eyes glossed over and my pupils narrowed, as I experienced a visual osmosis of the message. The images of several deceased soldiers – my friends – flashed before my eyes. I saw it, and by God, I felt it. The message: "Shon, live your life worthy of their sacrifices. – Debbie Lee."

My emotions and thoughts went into a thousand directions as if a hand grenade went off inside my head. My past dishonesty, lack of moral courage and integrity, those I harmed, my suicide attempts, and the chaos I created needed to be addressed. I wanted to save the world at that moment. I needed to make things right for my family, community, veterans, and God.

Accompanying the book and letter from Mrs. Lee was a copy of Marc's last letter home. Marc's letter emphasized "purity, morals and kindness." I realized I needed to bring closure to my crime – if there ever could be – by telling the truth, exposing my faults, and hoping that others could start to heal.

Taking Account

My first step was to admit all of my offenses, to the best of my memory, since alcohol was a contributor. I started by writing down the turmoil I put my family through. I compiled those events into a 10-page essay I titled, "Demobilization." I needed to tell the story and bring my wife back to life. Not only was she a teacher at a college of nursing, she worked in an emergency room on weekends. I'm a numbers guy. With Renee's untimely death, caused by me, there was a ripple effect in the universe. I had to account for every nurse she might have taught in her classes who would have gone on to save lives. Not only that, but also those she would have directly affected by working in the ER. Those are some big numbers. Her passion was helping others and now, I have to carry on her life's purpose.

Due to my felony conviction, I can't work in the medical field. However, I can share this story in the hopes of preventing other families from going through the same pain and destruction. So I called up a television station and agreed to admit what I did on the air, since I had told many lies about my wife in an attempt to justify my crime. I needed to start being a man and "worthy of their sacrifices" for our country.

My passion and zeal shot out of the gate like a bull, but I reconstructed my personal identity by showing love through service to others. I have to reorient my identity significantly with the limitations of being a felon. That message, in my heart, came from a multitude of sources;

Debbie Lee, Marc Lee, Renee, and God.

I now have a purpose, a mission and a lot of work to do.

Make Good Decisions

by Tran

Hello all our struggling youth. I hope and pray wherever you guys read this letter, that you guys make better decisions and choose a life away from the gangs. Let me share; life in gangs has appeal for many people. A sense of belonging to something, ideas that you have the protection of many others, and the easy solution as far as some money; by either selling drugs, doing other crimes, or being taken care of with what you need by other members of the gang. These are the attractions that seem great. No one thinks about doing things for other people and being used to carry out their personal ideas. Going to prison, getting hurt or killed, or getting your family hurt or killed; these things happen almost all of the time to people who get in gangs.

The only thing is that with some, it takes a lot longer to happen to them. Many look at the one guy, who is head of a gang, who has plenty of friends and money; eventually, the same usually happens to him, too. Even when it doesn't, there is the need to be constantly aware that someone might try to do something to him and his family and friends, because of his position in the gang. If there is one person that lives to an old age peacefully without a day in jail or prison, but is in agony, there is a much better dollar payoff then being him.

Remember that when you get involved with a guy in a gang, you sign on for a relationship with that guy, and everything that the guy has coming to him, even when you do not know what it is. Finding out about what you get later, is just about impossible to get out of. The bottom line is to ask yourself, "Is a relationship worth all of the other baggage you get from it somewhere down the line, maybe even years later?"

If you come into prison, you must realize there are many different types of personalities amongst you. Being respectful while also cordial, is a good trait to have and most likely keep yourself in a good frame of mind, as well as others around you! Regardless of what you have done or how long you have been or will be in prison, you're not a failure, unless failure is what you accept for yourself. In fact, it's impossible to be a failure if you use your time well.

If you've been in for a while, you know there are many ways to use your time well; continuing your education on you own, if a program is available; working toward a GED or college degree; participating in group counseling; attending self-help groups like:

1. Cage Your Rage;
2. C.G.A. - Criminal & Gang members Anonymous;
3. GOGI - Getting Out by Going In;
4. AA/NA;
5. PREP "Partnership for Re-Entry Program;
6. Donation Drive for Scholarship Fund;
7. Youth-at-Risk;
8. Groups that the prison may offer the community;
9. or getting involved with a prison ministry.

You can also work of developing and maintaining positive family ties and nurturing positive friendships or you can be a good friend to fellow inmates. By practicing stress-reducing techniques, like relaxation and meditation, you can support your emotional and spiritual wellbeing. You can also expand your knowledge and self-understanding by reading and studying certain books and articles. You probably know of others who have done this.

The essence of all time well spent is that it helps you experience the peace, dignity, and positive potential of your own true nature. Remember, no matter what is going on around you, you can experience some control over your own destiny. Also, you have to become more open-minded, as whole new worlds will open up right before your eyes.

Remember, you have to be the boss of your brain and no one can tell you what to think or what choice you make. Listen to those who have earned your respect, like your parents or anybody else who has given you real love and support. They are the ones that will support your decision, whatever it is.

What I Would Say to Someone Coming To Prison for the First Time

by Kevin Johnson

Understand, you have no friends here right off the bat. You will form relationships, even close ones, but the relationships will (or should) take time to develop.

Don't be too clingy. You will be alone, but being alone is not necessarily a bad thing. Remember, prison is full of criminals, but there are those who have come to the understanding that life as a criminal is not a life worth a damn.

Surround yourself with good people. Get involved in your institutional community events, e.g., the arts, music, theater, etc.

Be of service to others and you find joy and blessings.

Even though you're in prison, strive to be a good man.

Always introduce yourself with confidence, a firm hand, and eye-to-eye respect.

There will be those who will test you. Stand firm to your principles. Let your No's be No, and your Yes's be Yes. Don't wobble.

If you lack in education, take this time to improve your knowledge.

There will be a lot of distractions, stay focused. It is also easy to become lazy and complacent.

Stay busy! Staying busy will also keep you out of trouble.

Exercise. Working out reasonably will help you maintain a sound mind & body.

Keep your eyes on the prize. Understand, parole alone is not the prize. Lots of guys parole only to come right back. The prize is paroling a better man than you come in.

Sign up for Self-Help prison programs. Set your focus in self-help toward those programs that give you (or help you) gain a better understanding of who you are and how you got to be that person.

I'm not going to lie to you, taking a good long look at one's self is difficult. However, I have found that introspective analysis and assessment of self is necessary for true transformation of character.

Go back and identify, and then analyze those behaviors, thoughts and actions that gave you (or caused you) to turn from pro-social behaviors & activity.

Dig into your past and re-examine negative events and how you experienced them (what you felt), and your reactions to those feelings. You may see things differently now.

Understand that what works for our young selves in protection of our emotions, even if negative, we will likely repeat throughout life.

Rewrite your life script....

I also recommend journaling. It's good for the soul. It's also a kind of release.

Lastly, please use the name your parents gave your and not some silly made-up prison "handle."

Oh! And don't get tattoos. You're living the prison experience; you don't have to wear it for the rest of your life.

To All First Termers

by Anonymous

Please make this tour your last and your only tour. And, in the process, please, by all means, maintain your humanity and your sanity with due diligence, as your life depends upon it. Also invest constantly in the cultivation of your character. And learn to utilize your faculties, talents and gifts, to live a meaningful life of service. Further, and most importantly, do not allow racial, political, or the gang culture of prison, to cause a divide within yourself, or between others.

Incarcerated Men's Survival Guide

by David "Jazz" Brown

The idea of being one of the persons adding to the idea of the Incarcerated Men's Survival Guide continued to interest me until I finally did something about it. It made a lot of sense what I was hearing. A guide of a bit of information here and there, that has been not just said, but for the most part, lived. It is not a guide specifically for Veterans, specific ethnic groups, or aimed at any particular programming that has any portion to control. Instead, the Incarcerated Men's Survival Guide can provide you with information to give you a head start in certain areas. What you might want to look out for or perhaps, a positive and useful path followed by one or many that has been determined to be effective. My idea is to, perhaps, make you aware of certain things in advance, that I wish someone had let me know about before I ran head-first into it during the course of my incarceration.

For example: 1). I wish someone had told me that, because life moves on out there on the streets, to be on the lookout on how to deal with deaths that occur in the family. Most times, these deaths, or tragedies, happen all of a sudden. We have to be aware that, yes, life moves one. People pass away for a host of different reasons, most of which we cannot control. Being able to prepare oneself for this type of eventuality, is something I highly recommend. How do you do that? As hard as it might seem, just thinking about how we would react in sudden or untimely deaths within the family. Asking yourself the questions,

"Would it destroy me? Will it leave me at a point where I don't feel like doing anything anymore? Will my family be able to continue and function?" Then there is always the regret we feel for not being there to support family members due to the problems that you are having in your life.

To make a long story short, a couple of deaths in the family, slowed me down almost to the point of standing still. I blamed myself, my past lifestyle, my past irresponsible criminal conduct, that separated me from my family, that I am now continuing to have an impact on. All of these thoughts and more crossed my mind and heart during the loss of certain family members. I am just saying, be prepared to hold yourself up high and deal with these unexpected deaths, as they can, most times, set you back, or completely change the positive path that you were on. After having the deaths happen again and again, one right behind the other, I had to find a way to deal with it. What made it worse, is the fact that is makes you think of the lives and families that I impacted by my crimes, and we come to realize, that a life lost, is in fact, a life loss, no matter via natural causes or illnesses. In the end, the losses hurt; sadness and the fact that you will never see them again, turns into knowing what the departed person would have wanted for you after their sudden departure? Would they want you to stop? Would they want you to be completely consumed with grief to the point of negative, or possibly, graduated reckless and destructive behavior? No. We know we don't want that. The legacy they left is in us, and on a positive path, and finally, to live a life we know that they wanted us to have.

2). I wish that someone would have schooled me on the fact that I did not have to do things that I saw others do, just because I wanted to make myself socially acceptable to others. Having lived in the prison system from Juvenile stage and age, and now up past 60 years old, I can say one thing that I want you to hear; and that is: Be Your Own Person! Do unto others as you would have them do unto you, only, offer it to them first. Most men and women respect one another for having their own thoughts and decision–making processes, and on adjusting to what is right, and what is wrong within a closed environment, where bad conduct and behavior are seemingly expected; with disciplinary measures in place for such conducts. We know what's right and what is wrong. Our Mom's and Dad's did not miss that teaching on us. But when we see or know about the violations in here, we tend to let it go, or play the part of the innocent bystander, and just let it happen. Our Mom's and Dad's talk to us all the time. We just have to take the time to hear them. We are now in a place where we can do that over and over again……. Hear their voice and others, and instill those corrections in our lives.

3). Open yourself and make practice with each and every race and ethnic group that you can. In the prison system over the years, I have observed a mostly hidden and unmistakable power that lies in all that we are. When all ethnic groups come together on a concerted effort, to make life or the closed society that we live in better, cooperation's for all ethnic groups is what has always prevailed. That is part of what this Incarcerated Men's Survival Guide represents, learning how to reach out to one another. We can do that here and continue it out there. Let us touch the earth with gentleness, touch the earth with life, to reach out and touch and surprise life with the way in which we live today. We have been given the power and gift to create the world anew, if we touch the earth together, and let it start with me and you.

C.H.A.R.E.

by Juan Monroy

Ever since I started doing time in Juvenile Hall, I noticed I had trouble expressing myself and knowing what to write in letters. My shyness held me back on many levels, even conversing with others, and it showed up in my writing. Most of the time I would write one-page letters, and I'm not talking about both sides! Plus, I'm sure my letters didn't make a whole lot of sense. If only I would have had a guide or someone to let me know what to say or how to articulate myself in letters.

With that being said, are you interested in writing a meaningful letter to someone in your life? The letter could be to your mother, father, brother, sister, a pen-pal, girlfriend, wife, or anybody close to you which you would like to write. If so, please take the following into consideration.

C.H.A.R.E. is an acronym I came up to assist me with a format for writing letters. The acronym stands for Counselor, Humor, Art, Romance, and Educate.

Before I continue, I would like to express how C.H.A.R.E. came about. It started with a conversation back in 2008, while incarcerated with an older Mexicano in his early sixties, named Mousie, out of Los Angeles. We were at Ironwood State Prison, California, at the time. Knowing he was book smart and experienced in writing, I asked for his advice with correspondence, especially since I had trouble writing my then pen-pal. With his answers and my note taking, C.H.A.R.E. was born, of course, not in that exact order. I set it up in this fashion, so I could easily remember what I had just learned to apply it whenever I needed help with my letters.

Even though C.H.A.R.E. was designed to help me write my then pen-pal, not too long after, I realized the format could be used to write nearly anyone.

That's when I knew I was on to something.

Counselor: A counselor is a good listener, someone who pays attention to what the other person is saying. Repeating what is mentioned helps to let them know you are listening and understanding their point of view. A Counselor also gives advice through sharing personal experiences similar to what they are going through without actually telling the other what to do. If and when direct advice is given, be aware if something goes wrong the other person might blame you for following your advice.

Humor: Using humor usually results in smiles, laughter, and brightens a person's day. Here are a few examples you can use to cheer up their life. Jokes, cartoons out of the newspaper, funny childhood memories, or funny things that happen throughout the day.

Art: I'm sure everyone enjoys receiving gifts. Purchase a drawing or draw something yourself to mail out. Send out a hobby craft (if available). If neither is possible, decorate the letter itself with designs, stick figures, hearts, smiley faces, etc. (be creative).

Romance: Remember to comfort the other person by letting them know you care. Romance comes from the heart by being honest, sincere, and genuine. It is important to write thoughtful words that capture the other person's emotions. For example, "You make me feel appreciated",

"Your letter melts my heart", "Your words inspire me", "I miss you", "I love you".

Educate: Any learned information from a group, class, or program, may be educational for the other person. Whatever we see on TV that is inspirational and/or motivational, can also be shared. Anything positive we read can be enlightening. Imagine being able to teach someone something they might not know; it can be new and exciting to them.

For the New Guys

by Johnny Howe

My name is Johnny Howe and I have been in prison for 27 years, since the age of 17. I am going to share some things that were given to me, that have kept me alive. Before we get to that, there are a couple of things I want to invite you to continue to think about and ask yourself throughout the next 20 plus years that you will be spending behind these walls. First, who are the people who support you, write to you, come visit you, and go out of their way to take care of you? The next thing I want you to ask yourself is, what is it that you want to do once you are released, regarding the rest of your life? It may seem like a very long time away, but you will get out someday. Start working today, to accomplish those goals, and think before you do anything that may jeopardize them.

Although you may not love school, this is one of the things that will get you out of prison. Start working on your future today. Your education is something no one can take away from you and getting involved in school will keep you busy and out of trouble.

Another thing that I want to invite you to think about is how you became the person who did what you did to end up behind bars; so that you never make that same choice again in your life. Knowledge is power. The more you know about yourself, the more powerful you will become. I used to believe the man in my case died, because I shot him 5 times, but 20 years later I looked deeper and came to the realization that he was murdered by me, because I made terrible choices, and had poor decision-making skills. I was addicted to alcohol and drugs; I normalized criminal behavior through past crime; I had poor and unhealthy associations; I had extreme short thinking, and low self-esteem. I also had an unhealthy desire for attention and acceptance. I was selfish and had self-centered thinking. As a child, I had adopted distorted beliefs and traditions. I would like you to look over all these contributing factors that may have influenced your decisions and choices that got you in prison. The invitation is to, not only identify them, but begin to ask for help and work on them.

Remember, you won't be in prison forever. Look at this experience as a place to become who you always wanted to be. When I was on the streets, I worked hard, fought for things that never belonged to me, or that I would be able to obtain, such as a reputation; a street corner; a name, and how others would view me. Now I fight and work for better education, not only for myself, but others. I help others overcome their addictions to alcohol, drugs, gangs, and a criminal lifestyle. I do my best to do the right thing when no one is looking, and most importantly, I got out of my way to be of service to other people. I have come to realize that, unlike before; no one can take these things. What I would like for you to fight for, is your freedom, your family, and yourself. You have made some poor choices, but they don't have to define you or your future. You deserve a life worth living and another chance to be free and even though it may seem far off, it will come. How soon will it be up to you?

Now back to the rules that were given to me that I want to pass on to you:

1. Don't use or sell drugs (there's always a price)
2. Don't gamble
3. Keep your mouth shut and your ears and eyes open. Do you know why God gave you two ears and one mouth? So you can listen twice as much as you speak.
4. Don't volunteer and raise your hand to get involved in something that is none of your business, and could end up giving you another life sentence.

After serving two decades or more in prison, there are some common truths that we all come to, to find out to be facts:

1. The only ones who will be by your side throughout your time, will be your family. Homeboys will not write or come to visit for very long, if at all.
2. Things like education, values, integrity, and true heart felt relationships and the joy you get from helping others cannot be taken away.
3. True freedom is found within. You can find true freedom behind these walls if you truly look for it and that can never be taken away either.
4. Insanity is doing the same thing over and over and expecting a different result; and
5. Prayer is powerful and really does work.

These are all things that you will eventually come to find to be truths.

Remind yourself that this one terrible decision that you made that brought you to prison; does not have to define you as a human being. Educate yourself to define who you want to be. You can choose to do the same thing that you were doing on the streets and never get out of prison, or, get educated, attend self-help groups, find out who you are, and become the person you and your family can really be proud of.

Good luck! This road will be what you make of it.

Be Careful

by Anonymous

Once you come to meet people in prison, you will meet all types. Some will come to you and give you $20 or $30 of heroin, he will tell you to trade it for some canteen things that you may need, and you will do so. You'll get some soap, shampoo, something to eat, etc.

A month later, the same thing will happen. This man will give you heroin paper; $20 or $30 worth, here is where you get into the trap. Now you owe him. Next, he may ask you to take drugs to a cell or someone in the yard. He is not only testing you, he knows what you have done with the drugs, either you have consumed it or traded it. If you always trade it for things that you need, he knows you are not a user. Now he can use you to move some of his product. And, if he likes you or sees that you are not greedy, he will ask you if you want to sell for him; a few papers at first, then more. And now you are a drug dealer in prison.

Now, if he sees that you haven't traded it, he knows you are a user, through observation, he'll find out if your family helps you with things that you may need, money for the store, quarterly packages, TV, radio, all of this is money to the dealer. He'll give you a good deal at first and then he will take you for everything that you have.

Another way to get you to use drugs is to invite you to use with him. "Let's get high, bro," "Smoke this; it will make you feel good." He will dilute a small amount of heroin in a spoon, with a bit of water, and offer it to you, and say, "Come on, I don't want to get high alone." This is how it starts.

All of this happens with heroin-the most common drug in prison-or pot (cannabis), speed, sometimes they manage to get some other exotic drugs, but that is rare. So, be careful when you come to prison, not everyone who comes with a gift is your friend. They are just testing you to see how they can use you, if you don't end up as a client or a seller. You may end up as a mover, or worse. You may end up keeping the drugs in your cell or up your butt. You see the drug dealers rarely keep the drugs in their cell. Most of the time, they have a person who is a non-user keeping the drugs for them.

Getting caught with drugs can add a lot of time to your sentence. So be careful what you do when you come to prison!

(Untitled)

by S. Thames

When growing up, I used to hear all kinds of terrible stories about prison. Dangerous criminals; like robbers, murderers, and rapists. The convicted criminals pray on the weak and only the strong survive the challenges of an environment filled with hate, bitterness, and sorrow. It was a place I never wanted to go. Unfortunately, years later, I found myself in prison at the age of 18. I thought that I was a pretty tough guy from the streets and I knew how to handle myself. I was never in a gang, but I considered myself street smart! So I ran with that image to protect myself against the perceptions I believed prison was like.

Through my experience, I discovered that prison wasn't all of the terrible things I believed that prison was. Yes, it is a dangerous place to be, because the unpredictable can happen at any moment, so the one thing I had to learn, was how to survive it and make it home to my family.

When coming to prison, I learned the rules and regulations of what I can and cannot do. This is important if you want to go home on time, because in prison, some inmates just don't follow the rules. I made the choice that I wanted to go home, so I made the decision to not get involved with the things that I knew would get me into trouble; like drugs, alcohol, or any other criminal activity that prison can influence.

I wanted to change my life, so I had to change the way I thought about things and about myself. I wasn't a follower and minding my own business saved me a lot of trouble on my own journey of self-discovery. I am an optimist and I always moved forward with a positive attitude, because I believed in myself, and the ability to make a commitment to involve myself in everything positive to help me survive an environment that I believed was designed to keep me down. I found those like-minded, and we strive to learn what we seek to find; through education, self-help, and trades. This is how I found my way to survive this maze.

Why Does This Keep Happening to Me?

by Michael Nieto

Why does this keep happening to me? I asked myself this question several times throughout my 25 years in prison. See, I'm the guy that hits Rock Bottom, and then I pull out my shovel and start digging. So anytime I would act out, be violent, use drugs, drink alcohol, or be involved with criminality, I'd get a 115, SHU term, got to Ad-Seg, or the SHU.

Why does this keep happening to me? After 25 years, I've learned I created this belief system. It shaped my view of people, authority, and the world.

"IT" was "Happening to Me!" I had no part in it. I was the victim! Why isn't anyone else outraged over how I am being treated? Having this belief system gave me one of my justifications to be involved in my criminality, my gang activity, and my addictions. I loaded up my resentments, created more beliefs, more prejudice, more hate, and more crime.

I've learned that being willing to be wrong will change my life. I stopped saying, "It is what it is," "It's part of the game," etc. No, they were my choices and they were wrong. Nothing was "happening to me," that I did not put into motion, and carry out myself.

So, let me tell you young man, you don't have to live like a victim; you do not have to create distorted beliefs to justify your criminality; you do not have to be victimized; you do not have to go to the SHU for 10 years; you don't have to be charged in a Federal indictment. You do not have to experience all of this, to learn what I have just said… Because I did it already, for you and anyone else who will listen.

This experience taught me… Asking for help will give a new perspective, open you up to new thought beliefs; sobriety will give you, family, your tribe, a home, or a place to take the mask off. Being willing to be wrong, will allow you to be…Right, Authentic, and Honest.

I found being of service to others, will give me new feelings, and a new question, but you know the answer to this one now. Why does this keep happening to me? Because, I am of service, I'm honest, I'm sober, and most importantly, I am willing. So I get blessings, I get peace, I get friends, family, and … I get to feel good about myself. So, please give yourself a chance to be the real you! Not the perceived image. Care about yourself, not what others think, and be ready, cause people will cross your path that are there to help. Accept it, ask for it, and give it all you got! So you can give it to someone else.

(Untitled)

by Marlon Siguenza

I was incarcerated at the age of 21. Coming to prison at that young age was hard, especially since I came to prison with a double life sentence. For me, I had to choose early on to decide whether to go along with all that goes on inside prison and make that my life, or whether I was going to reflect upon my life history and choices and try to deal with the harm my past caused me and others, and now try to be someone who makes better choices.

Also, since the beginning I had to choose whether I was going to attempt to prepare for parole board by participating in self-help groups, vocational groups, and education; or not. At the same time, I had to choose whether I was going to try to appeal factors of my case, which meant I had to immediately begin to learn the law that applies to my case—to begin writing writs immediately, due to federal deadlines that now apply. As a result of the last 14 years, I have a record of ongoing programming, and even got a paralegal certificate, all while my case continues to move on in the court on the federal level.

Basically, if you're beginning your time, you have some real thinking to do as you decide how you want the next ... years of your life to look like while in prison.

While you litigate your case and prepare for board, prepare both mentally and emotionally for relationships to come and go, for loved ones that pass on or abandon you. Life goes on as usual while you are incarcerated. Now you have to choose how you will respond to life's events, whether, in a negative self-destructive way or with a new approach, based on new tools and experiences you may have gained.

And please, leave plenty of room for mistakes and failures. There will be plenty. Learn from all of them and persevere.

It seems to me, only God knows how our stories will end, as to how all the work we do now while incarcerated will come together. But the important part, it seems to me, is to do the work and go on the journey of self-discovery and growth – all while learning to be of service to others along the way, and making amends for our past mistakes.

Dear Beloved Blood Brother

by Dwayne C. Sims aka 'Elder D'

Greetings.

Word around town is that you are coming to prison for the first time. This has startled me, because I'm not used to knowing you for doing anything illegal and coming in contact with the law. Such as our sibling sisters, you have always been known to me to be one of the noble ones, and successful ones in our family. What happened to you? Help me understand your situation. Although I do believe that God allows all things to work for good for His reasonable purpose, this has also been such devastating news to me – and I assume others. Oh, well. What has happened has been done. It is what it is. There is no sense in crying over spilled milk, when all we have to do is grab a towel and wipe it up to be clean. Right! Anyways, I can't use it on cereals anyhow. Ha! Ha!

Not that I would promote prison to you nor anyone else, but prison does have its pros and cons, like everything else does in life. Since you are on your way to prison, let me share with you some knowledge, wisdom, and understanding I've learned myself, about this place and serving time. Hopefully, my words may encourage you to a life pleasing to God, yourself, and others; as you apply them to your life while incarcerated – serving your time.

Brother, I urge you to be strong and courageous, because you are going to need it. I've heard many people say that "only the strong-minded survives..." which I believe is to be a profound statement. Let faith and love in Christ guide your thoughts, protect your heart, build your character, keep you strong, and shape and mold you into the best person God will do to you – through you – for you, as you learn how to trust the Holy Spirit in your life.

Character is the key here and around here. Bearing good fruit (good works), tells us a lot about who you are around here. How you carry yourself around others; how you treat people; how you live in cells; are you a clean person (Do you clean after yourself?); how well you dress; how you speak, choosing your words wisely, it's what you say and how you say it and when is it the right time to say it…, who you keep around as company (whether a believer or not a believer); use caution!!!

The Bible says, "Do not be deceived: Evil company corrupts good habits." (1 Corinthians 15:33) Be mindful that all these things will help you live a life that is pleasing to God, yourself, and others – mostly to God. They will help you determine how well you will serve your time in prison until the day you are released from prison, and how well you will serve your community as well. Also, my brother, do you know that respect goes a long way. You have to give respect in order to get respect. However, although others may not return the same favor back to you, for your reward, you still show respect – by treating others the way you would want to be treated – returning "good for evil." For this is the peace of God. Those that tend to take your peace for granted – by taking your kindness for weakness – you being the bigger and better man, continue to show respect by holding your peace and gently close yourself with humility, humbleness, meekness, and love, and simply just walk away. It's not that you're putting yourself above that person, but that you are putting yourself above the situation.

Brother, do the best you can to eliminate the mess, the drama, and the games people play. Don't cause or go looking for problems that don't need to be. In fact, bring a solution about to each problem that finds its way to come against it.

Find yourself something productive to do, for this will eliminate the boredom of doing nothing constructive. Such things like: work (having a job), self-help groups, worship services, going to the library (do some reading), vocational trades (building your work skill knowledge), or if you need to, go back to school (get educated) while you're doing time in prison. All these things are great activities that will keep you focused on being positive in your community, in here –and-out in the free world, too.

Most of all… I encourage you to seek for a deeper spiritual life, if you haven't already. Establish yourself in the things of God. Create a personal and intimate relationship with Him. Learn to acknowledge and recognize the Creator for all of who He is, and for all that He has done – doing – and will to do. Let His blessings and promises interrupt your life, so that your salvation may be imparted to you, and understand that, hopefully, on earth that FAITH and LOVE is the key to life – and life more abundantly (Life Eternal that is!).

In conclusion, I hope this letter will find you in upmost respect of your purpose driven calling and cheer your spirit to do better with your choices in life.

All be the GLORY!!! And PRAISES!!! To God alone. Amen. P.S. My model is:

Love people, hate evil, and stay focused…

&

Be real, Be righteous, and Be relevant…

Sincerely,

Your Brother in Christ.

(Untitled)

by Vinh Nguyen

If you are reading this in a jail or prison cell, I hope you remember that tough time doesn't last only tough people do. I have been incarcerated for over 22 years and made many mistakes and bad decisions along the way. If I could go back and guide my 21-year-old self, I would tell him to truly reflect on who the most important person is, and what is the thing that he values most.

Whether it's your loved ones or freedom, let that be your anchor and do not lose focus when situations are stressful and challenging. It's vital to monitor your thoughts and behaviors to bring you closer to your family and freedom, rather than further away. It's equally important to ask for help. If you can identify someone whom you deem trustworthy of your trust, open up and share your inner thoughts and struggles. Take advantage of the mental health programs that are available to you and do not be discouraged by stigmas or by others.

Above all else, be kind and compassionate to yourself. No matter how much or how hard you judge and condemn yourself, it will not change the past outcome of what you've done. The sooner you practice forgiving yourself, the sooner you will be able to let go of the insidious belief that you are flawed and unworthy of redemption and good fortune in your life. Once you are able to truly reconcile and value yourself, you will be able to truly have meaningful relationships, especially the relationship with yourself.

It's imperative to nurture this relationship, because everything else in your life is influenced by this. When your internal conditions are aligned, all other external conditions, such as life's 'ups' and 'downs' can be constructively managed due to your clear and peaceful state of mind. It's also wise to take advantage of educational and vocational programs to continually improve yourself. I did not do this in the early years of my incarceration. Instead, I wallowed in self-pity and wasted many years drinking inmate-manufactured alcohol to escape reality. I regret that and hope that you will make better choices. Your future self will thank you.

Live your best life, no matter where you're at.

E.T.F.

by John Love

I am not a "people person,' but I will give you my rule of being locked up and being able to do your time by E.T.F.

E.T.F. stands for "Embrace The Fuck," which is what a friend who has now passed has named this way of living in prison.

If it's not yours, don't touch it. And don't even watch who does touch it.

If they don't call your name, leave SO alone because it will look bad if you're talking to them all the time.

Don't spend every second of your life thinking you know it all 'cause somebody always knows more than you.

You have 86,400 seconds every day of living in prison. You have to make the right choice for that day, 'cause if you choose wrong you will give someone else control over your life. Take your life into your own hands and leave all the B.S. behind. Think of the people who love you and respect them. Do your own time walking the line that CDCR has set forth for you.

I can talk 'cause I've been incarcerated for 29 years as I write this for you. I am at a place where I never thought that I would ever be, a Level One yard. Yes, I'm a Level One. I am doing this 'cause the two friends I had in prison wanted to do this to help you. And with them passing on, we, the people they helped are giving back.

Fuck your so-called homeboys, they don't care about you. If they really care, they will push you away, so you can get home to your family.

Always think before you act. If it don't seem right, it's not. Therefore, you should not get into it.

And if you know for sure it is right and you won't get into trouble, then do it.

Helping yourself is helping others.

Much respect.

What Could You Tell Someone Who Is Coming to Prison for the First Time?

by Seng (Kevin) Truong

I would tell him to challenge all his beliefs about himself and what his race tells him. Do you really have to follow the inmate's rules, or can you just do your own thing? Doing your own thing is getting a job, vocation or education, staying in the cell to study or going to the yard for exercising or playing sports. You can stay away from the politics if you want, because you can if you CHOOSE to.

What rules are you supposed to follow?

You are supposed to follow the rule of rehabilitation, anything that will change your own beliefs and actions, form negative to positive. Your family is counting on you to change and come home to them. You follow the rules of being a righteous person and everyone will respect you.

Where are you supposed to hang out at?

You hang out wherever you feel the happiest. Why would you be at a place of misery? Even walking the track alone is okay as long as you don't care what people think. You don't have to report to no one, it's your CHOICE to hang out anywhere.

How do you become involved in self-help groups?

All you have to do is ask and ask. Someone will lead you in the right direction. A lot of people are willing to help. Check the bulletin board in your wing. Help is just as simple as asking. Walk into a self-help group and the help is all around the room.

Incarcerated Men's Survival Guide

by Mark Marshall

In honor of the Veterans' Service Office founders Mr. Ed Munis and Mr. Michael 'Doc' Piper. Thank you for your guidance, as well as your selfless service. My friends… You are missed.

"What I'd Say to someone, who is entering the CDCR (Prison) for the first time: What not to do, and some guidance and advice on how to survive and rehabilitate ones' self."

Hello. My name is Mark. I'd like to take a little bit of your time and share with you a brief summary about myself, and the things I've been through doing time: "what NOT to do" (Negative lifestyle), as well as "what to do" (Positive lifestyle).

I began doing my sentence of 15 years plus a consecutive Life sentence, back in the 90's. I started out on the Level 4 yards, where I lived for many years due to my unwillingness to change, and continuous gang and criminal lifestyle. Prison then, was not like it is today. Back then, there was nothing for us to rehabilitate ourselves. Today, there are numerous self help recovery groups to involve yourself with, if you choose to do so. It's a wise choice to do so.

Coming into prison, I already knew to keep my mouth shut, and mind my own business, as well as to keep my eyes and ears on super-alert (hyper-vigilance), observing and listening to everything going on around me at all times. Being oblivious to your surroundings can be hazardous to your safety, and possibly your life. Always pay attention to what's going on around you, even when there's a "sign of peace" all around. Things happen… Quickly! Please stay vigilant. Living this way "twenty-something" years, has kept me alive and well in prison. Today, I've grown into a mature, responsible man, who makes positive choices in life. I didn't start out this way though.

When I came into prison, I was repeating the same negative thinking, attitude, beliefs, and behaviors. I continued living this way for many years in prison. Being in denial and not fully committed to confronting my issues of anger and impulsivity, alcohol and drug addiction, and my gang and criminal lifestyle, led me down the road of chaos and strife, which led to many "115's", "128's", SHU terms", and "DA referrals." I wound up picking up more time, in which this pushed my initial parole board date up by many years. I was very irresponsible, selfish, immature, angry, and extremely impulsive. I had become a despicable human being.

Today, I've outgrown all that madness in my life, because I truly desired to be a better person, and a responsible man, who controls his own choices in life. I desired to live a better life, and to do this, I needed to totally and completely transform myself... "inside and out." That's exactly what I did. I'll be straight up with you; this process wasn't an easy task. Being on the "level 4" yard, I didn't know where to start, or even how to go about it. I accept responsibility for not seeking any help of any kind. That truly hindered me, and hurt not only me, but my entire family and my friends in the community. I was a very prideful individual (negatively speaking), stubborn, and extremely selfish. I actually thought that I could rehabilitate myself – "by myself!"

When I reflect back over my life, I have so many regrets, such as not listening to my parents and sister's advice, regarding the people I began gravitating towards, and the places that I was hanging out at. I took my family and their advice for granted. I also regret not addressing my "character defects," as well as my "issues" while still in the community, before my life crime occurred. Back then, I wore a "suit of armor" of character defects, and created identities, that were driven by fear and insecurities. These defects drove me to do unspeakable things, that caused extreme pain and suffering to so many people, that is still being felt today.

I said all this to you because I care, and I don't want to see you go down the same self-destructive path like I chose to travel on, for my first fifteen years in prison.

So, with this being said, I'd like to now take this time, and give you some positive advice, and help guide you towards a positive pathway to doing time... pro-socially.

I hope that you will consider my brief experiences, of what NOT to do, when you're doing your sentence, whatever that may be. I wish you all the best in achieving your goals, your visions, as well as your inner freedom and peace of mind.

First and foremost, you must be respectful and considerate to ALL people: "correctional officers, free-staff employees, and to the people in the community" you are now living in. I know this is easier said than done, but do your best to display a good attitude, and have compassion for others.

I highly recommend that you stay away from ALL drugs and alcohol. Do not ever get anything on credit there's severe consequences behind not paying your debts. Also, do not borrow anything from anyone. If you do, you are responsible for whatever happens to it. If you break it, you bought it! This is a good time in your life to start practicing your patience. Do a lot of: reading, writing, or drawing, until; you purchase your own things. Believe me you'll avoid tons of drama.

I recommend that you read *The Four Agreements* by Don Miguel Ruiz. This book will open your eyes up on how to live life pertaining to these four agreements. Practice these daily. They're very powerful and valuable. The 1st agreement is "Be Impeccable With Your Word." This means, say only what you mean, and avoid speaking bad about yourself or of others; Do not gossip, because this usually creates rumors, which is bad – especially in prison.

The 2nd agreement is "Do Not Take Anything Personally." This one means don't let anyone's opinions, or actions of others affect you. Don't bite into an anger invitation. Be immune to this. What others say and do is a projection of their own reality. Use "forgiveness," to break the "cycle of revenge." This is a powerful coping tool.

The 3rd agreement is "Don't Make Assumptions." If, for any reason, curiosity consumes you, find the courage to ask questions and to express what you truly want, communicating with others as clearly as you can, will aid you in avoiding misunderstandings, sadness, regret, and extreme drama.

The 4th and final agreement is "Always Do Your Best." This one will change from time to time, depending on how you feel. Some days will be better than others, but no matter what, during any circumstances, just give it your all and do your best. By doing this, you'll avoid self-judgment and regret. These four agreements have helped me tremendously in my recovery, and in my life. I apply them daily as needed. I truly believe they'll be beneficial to you as well.

Next, be yourself – "all the time," whether you're out on the yard, your cell, dorm, etc. Do not pretend to be someone you're not. I've seen, as well as ran across a few "actors" in my journey in prison. To put it bluntly, "they don't act anymore!"

Character defects: these are negative character traits that we've created for ourselves. We create these identities to hide our true (usually afraid/scared) self from others, or situations we run across in life. The chief activator of our character defects is fear and insecurity. Character defects are a wall that we put up to guard ourselves from pain, fear, insecurities, shame, resentments, and guilt. All humans have them and no one is exempt from these "negative character traits." I would recommend that you learn what your character defects are, by working the 12-Step programs of either: "AA", "NA", or "C.G.A." (Criminal & Gang Members Anonymous). We develop these "defects" while growing up, and if we don't take the time to ask for help to address them, "they" will spiral out of control, and get us into some serious trouble. After you recognize and identify what your "defects" are, apply the total opposite of those defects into your life (positive character traits). A couple of examples, such as: "False pride," the opposite of that would be the principle of "humility." Humble yourself. Use humility and/or forgiveness, to combat false pride. "Aggression," you would use, "calm, peaceful, acceptance." It's not the same for everyone. Only You know what sets you off, also known as triggers. Learn all you can about "defects" and "Triggers."

Recovery programs…They're awesome! If you take your sobriety and recovery seriously, you will learn so much about yourself, and how to address and respond to the "issues" in your life. I'd like you to be aware and recognize any and all "high risk" situations for relapse, that you will encounter in here, whether it's alcohol, drugs, anger, impulsivity, as well as the gang and criminal lifestyle... and avoid or remove yourself as soon as possible. It'll be "temptation city," so beware of who you're around, and where you kick it at. It's all about choice. I truly hope you consider all that I'm sharing with you. Only you can stop the hurt.

There will be rules that you'll need to abide by. First, there are C.D.C.R. rules and then there's "our rules." This here is a slippery slope. Use your best judgment. You will decide one way or the other. I recommend that you follow the C.D.C.R. rules / policies. If you don't, there's many ways they'll punish you: "progressively." First, depending on the seriousness of the rule you broke, you'll be "verbally" spoken to by a "correctional officer," who'll give you a warning. The next level will be a "128-B" counseling chrono. Again, depends on the severity of the rule you violated. Finally, there's the '115' (administrative / serious) write-up. These are bad, and don't go away. Depending on the violation, and your part in the write-up, you'll lose privileges, such as: confinement to your cell, no yard, no phones, no quarterly packages, limited canteen, and sometimes – loss of appliances: TV, CD player, etc. A 115 may also get you a SHU term (Security Housing Unit). Solitary!!! Know this as well, just as in the community, your conduct in prison will come back to haunt you. So do the right thing, and remain disciplinary free.

To do this, find yourself some positive pro-social, individuals to hang around with, whether it's out on the yard, the dayroom, dorm, etc. Find someone positive and compatible that you can "cell up" with, who is not engaged in the criminal lifestyle. I realize that everything I've said to you so far will not be an easy task. However, I truly believe that your success will depend on the quality of those that you surround yourself with (accountability partners / support network). Surround yourself with positive, pro-social individuals, who truly believe in you, and whose goals and values are the same as yours, and who you can draw strength from. I'd like you to stay committed, determined, confident, and hardworking, at your rehabilitation towards sobriety, and recovery from your anti-social lifestyle and behavior, as well as addressing your "weaknesses" – whatever they may be.

I do understand and realize that this is a lot to do, changing your "ways" (negative lifestyle), but it's necessary to go through to achieve transformation, growth, and maturity. As a matter of fact, this challenge will be the greatest / hardest thing you'll ever face in your life. But, over time, it will get a little easier. You'll also feel better about yourself. Stay persistent, and through perseverance, you will prevail. You have a critical choice to make regarding your future.

Do this for yourself, your family, and your friends. In time, you'll be able to forgive yourself for your past, and once again, you'll be able to "love yourself." Always remember that there are people in your life who truly miss you, love you and need you out there with them… living honestly.

The sooner you get involved in self-help groups, the better off you'll be. If you're on a "Level 4," and there's a lack of programs, I recommend that you seek out some "correspondence" courses, thru the mail. "P.R.E.P. (Partnership for Re-Entry Program), or "Turning Point," are excellent programs to do, via mail. Their workshops cover: substance abuse, gangs, Domestic Violence, anger, etc. You can get their addresses thru your loved ones, building counselors, the yard chaplain, or a positive programming individual. Don't procrastinate. These "correspondence places" WILL write you back, and assist you. Seek help, and you shall receive it! Remember this as well…" you'll only get what you put into it." It's a lot of work, but very much worth it. Stay diligent. Stay busy.

Remember to apply all this knowledge into your life. It's called "internalizing," not memorizing.

Learn all you can about your character defects, your "internal and external" triggers: (things you "feel" inside of you; things: "outside of you). These things may contribute to a relapse. Knowing yourself well will be beneficial to you in prison, as well as in the outside community. Remember this always: Avoid & Remove yourself from "ALL" high-risk situations. Know what your "warning signs" for relapse are.

In time, you'll acquire peace of mind and ultimate freedom. Have a safe, successful, journey. I wish you all the best in your recovery. Take care, stay strong, and be safe.

With all my sincerity & respect.

(Untitled)

by Anonymous

I was 51 years old the first time I went to jail. This was in 2015. The first place I went was MCJ in L.A. County. It was a huge shock. I'm white. In California, racial identification in jails and prisons is imposed and strict rules are enforced by inmates on how interaction between races is handled. Failing to adhere to inmate-imposed rules is THE most likely reason to get assaulted in jail or prison. These assaults are carried out by members of your own race.

Fights between races is strongly avoided, because it instantly becomes a race riot, where ALL members of their given race are required to attack the opposing race. If you are seen as avoiding participation in such a melee, you will have a "price on your head" by members of your own race.

The rules vary some at different jails and prisons. In some jails and prisons in California, playing sports or cards, sharing food between whites and blacks, will get you in hot water, to say the least. Assaults are "ordered" and carried out usually by 2 or 3 members of your own race.

Sometimes these guys use shanks. I've spent 26 months in jail and prison, and I've seen a lot… The best advice I can give someone coming in for the first time is: (1) Learn the rules by talking to members of your own race; (2) Deflect attention; (3) Avoid accepting "favors"; (4) Read, read, read; (5) Respect yourself, other inmates and guards; and (6) Know that you'll survive and this whole horrible experience can make you a stronger and better person.

How Do You Deal With Medical?

by Anonymous

One subject that most people will not talk about to new people coming to prison is medical. Medical is one of the most critical things that should be talked about. I, for one, have quite a bit of experience dealing with medical. It took me over 5 years to get my hip taken care of. I had problems with it popping out of joint, starting in 2011/2012 and let my doctor know what was going on. He got me x-rays and told me nothing needed to be done. I kept at it with nothing getting done. I ended up putting in an appeal against my medical care. All I won was to get more x-rays.

I continued my pursuit of "medical care commensurate with community standards," as they are required by law to do. After 3 years of getting nowhere, I blew up at my doctor, because of the pain I was going through and his neglect of my care. That was a day like no other. He actually wrote a psych referral on me. Instead of listening to what I was experiencing and doing something about it, he instead, said I needed psychiatric help, not medical help.

When I did speak to the psychiatrist, she agreed with me, in that, I should have been upset for them not doing something. Finally, after 4 ½ years, I got an MRI, which showed the hip had deteriorated beyond repair, and now, needed to be replaced. When I confronted my doctor about him not doing something sooner, he stated that, I am not supposed to spend money on treatment that is not needed. I also told him, that if he had done something sooner, I would not have needed the hip to be replaced.

Finally, after 5 ¾ years, I finally got the hip replaced. I only give you my story to let you know that prison medical care can be lacking in so many ways. They are continually told not to spend any money on inmates' care. They

90

don't want to do anything to help. The doctors that do care, and try to do something to help are berated by higher ups and told to stop doing anything that costs money. You will have to be your own advocate when it comes to medical care. Be proactive on your own behalf, otherwise, nothing will get done.

Do you care about how they treat you? If something is wrong with you physically, do you want to be taken care of? Or do you want them to get away with doing nothing to help you? One of the things that I didn't mention earlier was that I even had to file a complaint with the California Medical Board against my doctor. Now, that really got to him and he really was afraid of what might happen if I was able to tell them the truth. He tried to do little things that wouldn't help me, but, by his thinking, would mend the rift between us. I, in no way, was going to let him squirm out of what he had coming from them. In fact, I had to file another complaint about a year after the first one.

BE PRO-ACTIVE for your medical care. They don't care about you. All they care about is the bottom line, dollars! Make sure you follow up on any and all medical issues you have. I can only speak for myself, but I want to have my medical needs taken care of, how about you? Don't give up when they won't do anything or you can't seem to get anything done. That's when you have to fight the hardest on your behalf. Don't let them win the battle. You want to be the victor in the battle for your healthcare and make them spend the money they get to take care of you properly.

The term, "commensurate with community standards," is the key statement to use when you're battling them. If people on the streets are getting medical care for the same thing you are going through, then they are required, by law, to do the same kind of treatment for you. Follow up on everything that is done. Make sure you make them give you the results of all testing; x-rays, blood tests, MRI's, CT Scans; well, everything you have done! You get the picture of what I'm getting at. Your healthcare is in your own hands in prison. If you don't care if they take care of you, then forget what you've just read, but if you do care, make sure you do something.

What Are You Going to Do When Something Is Wrong with You?

by Kevin L. Webb

A Constitutional Level of Adequate Medical Care?

Okay, so you found yourself in prison. Now what? Let's talk medical. Your care; treatment; options; truths and fallacies, regardless of what you heard, inmates do not receive the gold standard of treatment people do on the streets.

Under the U.S. Constitution, you are only entitled to "adequate" medical care and treatment. It's hit or miss. Some PCP's are good, most however are dump trucks that couldn't make it in the real world.

When it comes to protecting and advocating for your health, you are the captain of this ship. You want quality health care? Guess what, 9 out of 10 times, you are going to have to fight for it.

In 2008 I was diagnosed with a tear of my superior labrum in my hip. Finally, in 2010 after seeing a specialist, arthroscopic surgery was ordered. It was promptly denied by the Chief Physician and Surgeon.

What originally would have been a 90-minute outpatient surgery, 3 months on crutches and life would go on, turned into a 9-year court battle which ultimately resulted in my needlessly losing my natural hip due to the time I was forced to go without ANY treatment or adequate pain management. Finally, after being evaluated by 4 expert orthopedic specialists, it was determined that my hip condition deteriorated so much that the only option was to perform a total hip and joint transplant. Imagine that, 9 years without adequate treatment. Well, any treatment.

I was totally ignorant to the law or medical policy/procedure until I arrived at CTF. Thus my education began. I hope I can impart some wisdom to you my learned reader.

When it comes to your health, don't mess around, if you can't get adequate treatment for whatever ails you, get ready to fight and push the issue. Whether it be submitting multiple health care requests, appeals, family calling, letters to legal organizations, medical boards, etc.… Stay on top of it and DO NOT LET IT GO! The medical department is banking on the fact that when you start a fight, you'll easily give up and dismiss your claims. Stand your ground, even if it means going to court.

In my case, a $65k surgery turned into a $250k surgery. Legal fees alone cost that much. All to tell me no to something that was medically necessary,

Whatever chronic care condition you may have, make sure you address and get it treated. Again, if you run into road blocks, push the issue.

Beware of the prison doctor who pushes pills on you for whatever condition you may allegedly have. In my case, I took blood pressure and cholesterol medication for over a decade. Come to find out, I had neither condition. If they say you have something you believe you don't, make them prove it to you.

There is one factor you must pay close attention to if you are in the California Prison System. It's called "HIGH RISK MEDICAL." This classification was supposedly initiated to lump specific medical risked inmates into institutions which could best handle their medical needs. In theory it sounds great. However, in reality it is a joke.

For instance, if you are 65 years old, you are automatically classified as high risk medical. Even if you have the physic of Jack LaLane and an iron constitution. You can be forcefully moved to an institution which will do absolutely nothing for you than what is being done at your current location. A transfer is fine for the inmate who requires specialized care. If you don't, you have the right to fight it! Inmates have sued in court over this issue and won under age discrimination and forced the department to return them to the institution which they were originally housed.

You can be placed on high risk for taking too many medications or having specific medical conditions. Whatever the case, if you are classified as high risk and you have no apparent symptoms requiring your transfer, fight it!

When it comes to a medical condition which will require surgery and you are getting a lot of resistance, whether it is refusal to diagnose and/or treat. Create and maintain a paper trail. This is of utmost importance should you be required to appeal the matter or litigate it in the court system. Evidence is your best friend. The more you have in your favor, the more apt the court will rule in your favor and provide the relief you are requesting.

If you have any doubt about yourself and your condition, what treatment, etc., you are entitled by law to review and get copies of your medical records. I highly suggest as a rule (if you have any chronic care conditions) to regularly review your medical record and get copies as needed. The doctor isn't always telling you what's going on with you. That's why it's best to review the official record so that if there are ANY questions or doubts, they can be addressed. Always remember, medical records are legal documents which can and are used in litigation. For and Against you. Please allow me to illustrate a situation for you which, in itself, is another important issue.

If you ever have to refuse a medical visit, treatment, procedure, transportation, medication, etc.… IF you are offered a medical refusal slip to sign, DO NOT SIGN A BLANK SLIP. Make the staff fill the form out COMPLETELY in front of you before you sign. If you are not allowed to complete the form, refuse to sign it and immediately do the following upon return to your housing unit.

1. Fill out a medical request stating the exact reason why you refused (whatever it was you refused) and request follow up appointment.

2. File an appeal against the medical staff for refusal to allow you to fill out the form and falsification of a legal document.

A refusal form is a legal document. Make sure it is filled out correctly; in front of you. If not, request a nursing supervisor or custody to document their refusal.

The bottom line, you are in control of your health care or lack thereof, the prison system is only concerned with keeping you alive so they can make money off you. Request treatment for conditions requiring treatment. If dissatisfied, initiate the appeal process. Maintain a paper trail, question everything. If it's not needed, don't take it. If it's required, push for it. And if needed, litigate it. Sometimes the prison system only understands a court order. You are in control of the quality of your health care, and you alone must make the decisions to maintain the quality of life you desire so that when that parole date arrives, you walk out of prison in good health.

To Those Who Come to Prison after Me

by Raul Garcia

Before I begin, let me give you a quote: "Everything can be taken from a man but one thing; the last of human freedoms-to-choose one's attitude in any given set of circumstances, to choose one's own way."

The first thing that I would say to you is that you need to stop and recognize that your life isn't the same as it was and neither are the lives of those connected to you. Because of that, you will need to be flexible in your thinking and actions. Know that you brought yourself here and it isn't at the price of anything of yours; the people who are praying and will continue to pray are those closest to you and those believing that you will someday come home. Coming to prison is a selfish act, so you should think of how to reverse that way of thinking, because you are only hurting those who care about you. Not only that, but you are wasting life and someday you will look back and regret not utilizing your time better. If you are a father, then you really need to pay attention, because this time in your life (if you are close with your children) will mold and remake their way of thinking completely. Worse than them having to see you in prison is the times that you cannot be present for those pivotal moments in their lives.

The one thing that will be a constant in your entire stay in prison is that you are not in control and that the program will change without notice. This will be a continuous lesson in patience and hopefully a reminder that you are not the center of the earth. Doing time now, (in this era) is not the same as it was prior to your arrival, so with that in mind, do not try to live according to the past or previous ways. Do not live in the "past," that time is gone. Do not beat yourself up and ask yourself, "what if." The thing you need to focus on is living in the here and now, analyzing the past (only to recognize our defects), and using that understanding to create a future that will be progressive and positive.

Here is another quote: "People sacrifice the present for the future. However, life is available only in the present. That is why we should walk in such a way that every step can bring us to the here and now."

Ask yourself this; what do I want my time in prison to be like and do I want to go home? I know everyone says that they want to go home, but you will see that is not always the case. Because of the convict community, many feel they have to do as others and consequently end up doing more time or not leaving at all based on someone else's ideals and belief system. Therefore, as you read this; I implore you to ask yourself who are you truly and are you strong enough to do your time boldly as just yourself. You are responsible for all your choices and need to be willing to accept the consequences (good or bad). In short, it is time to grow up and start valuing others, before yourself. In order to do that, you must recognize the value you should be placing on yourself. If you look and realize that your self-value does not exist, then you need to do some serious introspection. You cannot love others if you do not love yourself, just as you will not value others if you don't/won't place value upon yourself.

Quote time:

"A man's character is the reality of himself.
His reputation is the opinion others have formed of him.
Character is in him; Reputation is from other people-
That is the substance,
This is the shadow."
—*Henry Ward Beech*

One of the hardest things to come back from is when we feel that we failed to reach or accomplish a goal that we set forth to obtain. I hope that as you do your time, you will come to the conclusion that you have to make some adjustments to the way you think, which in turn will affect your behavior. If you do not think that this is true, take a look around you; was this place in your plans? As you do this, you will find yourself caught up in the whirlwind of change. This is when you need to ground yourself, if not you will burn out, or the weight of everything will bear down on you until you quit.

I have another quote for you to meditate on: "We all falter and from time to time and slip below the line of self-expectation; when that happens, remember that our life and the changes we are attempting, are work in positive progress, and we can't allow ourselves to get caught up in the toxic expectation of perfection.

In a nutshell, what I am trying to say is that the minute you get to prison (hopefully this will already be a thought), you need to think about what kind of person you are, what kind of person you want to be, and what kind of person you intend to present to your new community. The person you are is the one that you present to yourself when you are all by yourself. The one who allows the defenses to come down (removing of the masks). The one that is vulnerable and open to experiences of life, curious even. Most likely, the one we see at visits, once again being the child as parents or loved ones come and visit.

The person you want to be is the one that has insight into why you are here and understands the tremendous damage being so selfish has caused so many others. This person recognizes that his life can only go one of two ways: ONE, being what you're currently experiencing and deciding to make this kind of life a "career," all because you want the world to revolve around you. Or TWO, this person finds true remorse for not only the people hurt in the commitment of your crime (every crime hurts someone in some fashion), but all the people throughout your life that you recognize your actions have affected in a negative way. If you find this person in yourself, you will experience many things you never have and possibly many things you have to put away at a younger age, because of some kind of trauma, neglect, or abuse.

The person you intend to present to the community is the one that will set the tempo with those around you. This is the person you will most likely find yourself presenting, because it is the one with all the defenses (not always true, for some have never been in this kind of situation or environment) put in place. A few things to pay attention to are: FIRST, remember there are people who have been here for a long time and can read a phony. This could be bad for a couple of reasons; it can either get you alienated or possibly mark you as a potential victim, because you will be recognized as a "fish," or worse, a liar. SECOND, there are some that look for people just like that; they are a type of predator that befriends you in order just to use you or your resources.

Most young people come to prison with the persona of being "tough," because of the fear they are experiencing at this new environment and the sudden turn of events that now mark what is your life. The thing I think is the most dangerous thing about presenting a persona to the convict community is that it could come become "stuck," or worse, forgotten that it is a persona. This happens because the persona is worked on and shaped until it fits like a second skin, that allows you to have a small sense of safety and it is ideal to hide behind in so many ways. The persona stops a person from development though, because all energies are put into shaping, molding, and readjusting it in order to keep you safe (physically, emotionally, and mentally). I want to share a writing that rather presses my point of the persona and how it can be dangerous.

"Irrational Fear Harms Mental Health"

People who experience long-term hyper-vigilance may have unintended negative mental health consequences, some scientists say.

Remaining in this state of very hyper-vigilance can contribute to issues like social anxiety, hypochondria, post-traumatic stress disorder, insomnia and all manner of phobias," according to an article in the Wall Street Journal.

The amygdale is responsible for the feeling of fear. It primes you to react – quickens your pulse, creates muscle tension and dilates your pupils when you sense danger, according to Ahmad Hariri, a professor of psychology and neuroscience at Duke University.

The amygdale served us well as cave dwellers warning us of lions and lurking tigers, but it can get in the way of our modern life. "Change has occurred so rapidly for our species that now we are equipped with brains that are super sensitive to threat," said Hariri.

For some inmate doing time, being locked in a cell for days at a time is normal.

Sometimes, they use the time productively like studying, reading, or exercising. Inevitably, with extra time on their hands, the mind may wander to family-friends or their future, causing stress and fear. "Remaining in this state of wary hyper vigilance can contribute to issues like social anxiety, hypochondria, post-traumatic stress disorder, insomnia, and all manner of phobias. "We essentially drive ourselves nuts worrying about things because we have too much time and do not have many real threats on our survival, so fear get expressed in these really strange, maladaptive ways," said Hariri.

To calm and overactive amygdale requires admitting unease and fear, the Journal reported. "You are actually stronger if you can acknowledge fear," said Leon Hoffman, so-director of Pacella Research Center at the New York Psychoanalytic Society and Institute in Manhattan. On the flip side, when someone ignores their feelings of fear, they may compound the consequences.

"The more you try to suppress fear, either by ignoring it of doing something else to displace it, the more you will actually experience it," said Kristy Dalrymple, a clinical assistant professor of psychiatry and human behavior at Alpert Medical School of Brown University. Healthy coping skills to reduce fear:

- Talking to someone you trust about your fears.
- Remembering that you are loved or could be loved.
- Actively engaging your analytical thinking.
- Sense and appreciate the fear.
- Having a commitment to overcome fear that is consistent with whom you want to become.

—John Lam

Therefore, my point being, do not go in as something you are not and risk the consequences of that decision. I know it's not always comfortable just being yourself, especially if you're used to being picked on; but believe me, after whatever time it takes for you to come to the realization that the only real way to get out of here (especially after you realize how hard it is on those who love you), you will need to work on yourself. In order to do that you have to experience things as yourself and make the necessary changes in the authentic you. Remember, if you can be yourself, all your energies can go into transformation.

Being in prison is 90% mental and 10% physical, but that mental part can be tough. If you can mentally endure prison, you can pretty much endure in most places and with most people. If you are serious about mentally conquering yourself and your environment, you have to keep an open mind in all things at all times. If not, you will at some time miss something that you need to know because that old inner critic will be too loud for you to hear anything else. Last thing, when you are being influenced to do something that can potentially put you or your freedom in jeopardy, stop and look at your I.D., you will notice that there is only one person in the picture. That one person is the same one who will either take the hit and suffer the consequences for a situation (usually one that has nothing to do with that person), or that person will be the one courageous enough to stand on his righteous principles (that he learned through his transformation) and eventually be walking out the door…by himself.

Segregation and SHU Syndrome

by Michael Nieto

As I sit today, I've been in prison 26 years and 7 months. I spent 10 years in the Security Housing Unit (SHU). I want to address the thoughts, feelings, and beliefs, that came up for me while in segregation.

I am a child of abuse. I was exposed to severe, extreme violence in my home. I was the one being attacked by my brothers and my parents. I identified and created the belief system that, ONLY violence can deter my victimization. Holding on to the belief, maintaining this belief, allowed me to justify my criminality, and create a victim mask. "Why do they keep picking on me? I didn't do anything. They're out to get me." I would never admit what I was really doing.

In isolation, I feel immediately threatened. I feel unsafe every day. I perceive the immediate threat of violence is everywhere, all the time. My anxiety rose to unbelievable heights if the perceived threat is real or not.

Let me give you an example. After I was released to CTF-Soledad, directly from the SHU; within weeks I was diagnosed with shingles; brought on by stress anxiety; a physical manifestation of extreme pain, due to my anxiety, which was a result of segregation.

A key trigger for me is "keys." I hear keys and I believe "They're coming to get me!" I start to get in my head, anxious, nervous, or threatened. I jump up; stand on the door looking out, If I have contraband or not. It is my normal. It was not pretty being myself; in a cell with nothing. It is a form of torture. To experience it for a decade was inhumane.

To have someone wake you up every 30 minutes (sleep deprivation tactics), moving you from cage to cage, cuffed and shackled like an animal; you start to feel like one. It is very difficult to maintain a piece of yourself or a connection spiritually. The SHU is designed to cut off all sensory deprivation, to break you.

Being a victim of violence in my home, I lost my sense of safety, hope, and my innocence. When I went to segregation, I began to feel these feelings again. The thoughts began to creep back in...

You're worthless, you'll never be anything, no one loves you, you're not man enough, you're a girl. I began to push hope, faith, love, my feelings, emotions, and myself, way deep down. In my own lil SHU cell, if you will, inside of me.

I was making horrible decisions, choices; I was deliberately not dealing with stressful events, deaths, or my own actions. I created a "Victim Mask." I would wear it for the next 25 years. I was actually insecure, afraid, depressed, inadequate, terrified, resentful, hurt, angry, ashamed, and vulnerable; I was sad, I had feelings of abandonment, and no tools to deal with how I felt. So I am super anxious, afraid, and inadequate, having these feelings, and thoughts. I was impressionable and willing to be violent, to gain acceptance and recognition. I was willing because I didn't feel masculine enough. My idea of a man was violent, unapologetic, apathetic, skeptical, distrusting, and cunning.

I had low self-worth and poor peer association. I solve problems by using violence, not to mention I am an alcoholic, addict, and a gang member. I made decisions by choosing violence first, and making myself the victim; second, then becoming resentful; third, so I can ultimately justify my criminality, addiction, and violence, by making myself the victim. The beauty of choice is; you can change them in any moment. I decided I needed to take care of me.

I got married, I realized people care about me, I got sober, I started participating in Mental Health, I started thinking about consequences, talking about my pains, hurts, I get emotional, I got real. I found by talking, writing, sharing (honestly), and trusting people, I found a community, a safe place, to ... feel. I began to make positive choices, choosing peers that also hold my best interests at heart, I went to groups; AA, and I started being REALLY HONEST working with sponsors. I started donating my time to be of service, to work the 12-steps, in every part of my life. I began to feel hope again in myself, in the world, and I began to feel really proud of myself.

We all have pasts, hurts, and choices. I want you to know you are capable of making good choices. You don't need to go to the SHU. You don't need to act out to get help. You can seek our help, put yourself first, your families, and your freedom.

I sincerely hope you can find a piece of you in my story, and know you are OK. You are of worth. People care about you. There is a lot of help, you just have to ask, take a step, to help you get home, to help you, For You!

Dealing With Death While Incarcerated

by Richard Ranta

While serving a term in prison, many of us will have family or close friends that will pass away. These times can be particularly hard on you. I have lost my parents and sisters while serving this sentence. I have also lost about 25 friends. I had a close relationship with all of them and it really hit me hard. I've also dealt with family members battling cancer and accidents. They had chemo, radiation, and surgeries, to combat cancer or other major injuries. I wasn't able to be there for them. I couldn't talk to them on the phone. I've found that most prison staff couldn't care less about what you're going through. Most of them won't show you any compassion or empathy towards your situation. This is something that you will most likely to have to do on your own. So, you have to be prepared to have a way to grieve and move forward with your life. Life doesn't stop because of death. Life goes on. You have to move on.

It might not be easy, but you have to focus on yourself and the future. We all grieve differently. I isolated myself in my cell and stayed away from everyone for periods of time. I found that that was one way for me to deal with it. Of course, that is not a good way to deal with it. When I lost my mother in 2010, my counselor sent me a post it with a phone number on it and wrote that I should call that number. He then went on vacation for two weeks, leaving me with no way to contact my family. His job was to get me on the phone, so I could at least talk to my family about who died and when. At times like this, you need others to help you get through the ordeal, especially your family.

The second way I found to deal with it is to have a relationship with God. I pray, I read the Bible, and do correspondence Bible studies as a way to deal with it and many other things. I have also learned meditation. This helps me stay focused on what I need to do to continue my journey.

This can be done to deal with death or to work on getting out of prison.

These things help me sort through the many feelings that come when someone passes away or is severely injured. I know that most of us don't get visits. Visits can be helpful in dealing with death, but for some, it might make it worse. Your family or friends are there for just a moment in time. If you don't get visits, you won't have that fresh image of that person bouncing through your head all the time, but it might help you to through the process of grieving. We are all different and have learned our grieving processes while we were growing up.

I've found that death is a part of life. We live, we die. There is nothing we can do to change that. All we can do is to move forward with our lives. We can't get stuck letting ourselves stay focused on the death of someone we care or cared about. Life does move on and we have to learn to accept death as part of life. It can hit us hard and we might not think that we can get past it, but we can. Yes, it hurts. Sometimes a death will hurt it worse than other times. Sometimes, we might think the hurt will never end. It does! It might take some time, but you will get through it.

Life does go on and we have to move on from that experience. It's not forgetting about that person, but remembering the life you shared with them, the good times, the bad times, the sad times, and the happy times. I've also learned to celebrate the life of that person, not the death. If you share the good things in that person's life with others, and think of the positive things you've experienced with them, it is a way of dealing with it, staying focused on your future.

You can get through it by being of help to others. I made a choice to come to work in the

Veterans Service Center. The motto of the office is "Helping Ourselves by Helping Others."

I've found that by helping others, I am actually helping myself at the same time. I have also learned to follow what the golden rule, "Do unto others as you would have them do unto you." By thinking of others instead of yourself, the focus of the death is put on the back burner of your mind. Your focus is on the work you are doing. Accomplishing some positive things will tend to bring your focus to the present and not reliving the past.

Another way to deal with death is to do things in honor of that person. This gives you positive reaction to something negative. It gives you a goal to work for. It's something to keep your focus on; something positive, something good in your life. The main focus should be to live! Your life is not over. Your life is moving forward. So LIVE!

No Matter Your Situation

by Raul Garcia

Let me start this by saying this truth: I want you to recognize that no matter your situation or how you feel about it, today is not the end. In fact, if you want it to be, it can be the beginning of a process of change that forever will change you to the core, and alter the way you used to think. This will not get you home, keep you out of prison, but also actually change your perception and in turn, enrich your life.

This is my second try at trying to express concern and to provoke the readers of this, to expand their mind and consider change sooner than later. I do this as I assume others do too, because, through my time incarcerated in State prisons, I have learned some undeniable truths. To me, these truths are important and key to unlock mental and emotional growth, that will facilitate necessary change and allow me to walk out of prison. I am trying to save the reader the time (which is a unique and priceless gift), struggle, pain, and much new uncomfortable adjustments to my core beliefs I had to go through. Granted, the reader has to do his own work, but there's no reason myself and others can't provide a roadmap. So, on to my thoughts for this second entry... Since we are on the topic of change on so many levels, one of the core questions you should probe into is: honestly, what got me into prison? Do you know why there is only one picture on your I.D.? It's because you got you in prison. This is truth-whether you care to believe it or not now it's either time to grow up or lay down and die for the system's benefit. One important aspect of self-realization is that we have to be honest with ourselves, and look at attributes, such as; responsibility and empathy; tools, such as: comfort zones, coping skills (both positive and negative), and those things we do to avoid having to do with what got me to where I am today.

Self-realization is not easy, but I encourage it because, you don't have to worry about what others may think on this process. The results though, are another story. They occur regardless if you want them to or not, but the benefits from them are truly worth it.

For those without Life terms, ask yourself this question, Do I really care to analyze why I'm in prison and who/how that affects all those that, not only care about me, but my impact (both in prison and on the streets) on all those 'connected' to me? Truthfully, this is a question I had to always face, because of my life term. It didn't occur to me until I had spoken to several non-lifers in many different settings; that this is one of those questions that relate more to one group than another. This question is important because it's one a lot of lifers constantly are faced with, and eventually, we are faced to answer it because of growth, upcoming Boards, or maybe, it's a topic in self-help group and therapy. As we learn to face it, we are confronted with learning that we are very selfish, and that, in order to get out of prison, we need to change (mentally and emotionally). We learn that it usually takes around ten years to discover this need to change and grow (in order to get out and more importantly, stay out). So, for a non-lifer, this question is really about how selfish you are (honestly) and if not being selfish, how my actions alter the lives of those in my life (sphere of influence), whether you know them or not. In addition, it's a gut check to see if you really give a damn about getting out and staying out. Me, personally, I can't stand prison (the food, the living conditions, having to shower with men, the constant B.S. and drama), but if you're a short timer, and you always enjoy doing the installment prison plan, I encourage you to think on my words.

So, what truly are my priorities, and why do I feel they are chosen to be more important than other things, or people in my life? For me, on a daily, minute-by-minute reflection, I am faced with asking myself if these "priorities" are really my priorities, and are they really important to me. What about you as you read that? Are you taking care of your priorities? If so, I challenge that, by asking how that's really possible while you are in prison.

After priorities, I would ask myself about what loyalties are. What specifically are mine (self, gang, God, family, friends, no one, etc.) and how did they become my loyalties. Just like priorities, look and see if you are really taking your loyalties serious, and how am I showing my loyalties to they/it. A lot of times we create these personas that we issue these loyalties, and state what its priorities are. Here's the thing though, that persona isn't really you, and it's probably one of many coping tools and defenses that, at one time, you felt the need to create. So, what happens if you removed any persona that you might be wearing, and then ask yourself the questions I have posed? I can almost guarantee that your answers would be different. Maybe even significantly different, depending on how deep and honestly you searched for that truth.

All the things that I have posed so far are just beginning stages to ultimate change. That change, is one that many in prison, and even on the streets avoid, even acknowledge exists, until they are put in an environment where no one has to or can be, genuinely self, and accept its visage in the mirror.

Last part, we are almost done. Can you now truly envision who you really are, and who you really want to be? This one's hard for many people, because of their 'associations', and the consequences of being a free thinker, and desiring to be something more as an individual. Where will you be and what condition will you be in (mentally, emotionally, physically, and financially) next week, next month, shoot, what about later this day. Question yourself why this question is even important.

That's it folks. Another little bit of hard-earned wisdom from me. You don't have to take it, you don't have to agree with it. Man, you don't even have to like it. If that's the case, then I want to know one final thing. Why did you read to this point then...?

Truthfully, I and other lifers want to see others go home (even if we don't), because as we sit day by day, the hard understanding of empathy, slowly removes the crust we have surrounding our ability to experience compassion. That compassion combats our selfishness, and drives us to not only enlighten those that arrive in these iron houses, but attempt to help others learn how to break the cycle of multigenerational dysfunction. This ailment is one of the major causative factors of incarceration for men.

Reflections on 'Living Sober' by following Alcoholics and Narcotics Anonymous

by Anonymous

Alcohol and drug addiction have a psychological effect that changes our thinking and reasoning. Example: we think we can handle another drink or shot of dope, and we feel we can tolerate another then another. In our distorted thinking, we believe we can drive. If you don't take the first drink, you can't get drunk, and if you don't take that first shot of heroin then your sobriety gets stronger. One drink or shot of dope is too many; but twenty drinks are not enough. The insanity of alcoholism and drug addiction is we think we can handle it and control our usage.

That's why our lives become so powerless and unmanageable. Doctors who are experts on alcoholism and drug addiction explain there is sound medical foundation that if a person is addicted to alcohol or heroin, he must not take that first drink or shot, because even one drink 'triggers' and one shot of heroin 'triggers' the compulsion to continue using or drinking more. Recovered alcoholics or addicts often say "just stopping is not enough". We need to implement positive programs of action—we have to learn how to live sober. Alcoholics Anonymous (AA) and Narcotics Anonymous (NA) are 12 step programs which have had great success in helping any addict or alcoholic do just that—learn to live sober.

AA and NA prayer: *"God grant us the serenity to accept the things we cannot change, the courage to change the things we can, and the wisdom to know the difference".*

The first step is to admit we are powerless over our addiction. The American Medical Association has noted that "a treatment of this condition primarily involves not taking that first drink or fix". By admitting we can't control this illness by ourselves, we become willing to do whatever it takes, whatever steps are necessary, not to drink or use. We have viewed alcoholism and addiction as a life or death matter.

We can't do this alone we need fellowship and the support of people who have been in our shoes to help guide, support, and encourage us. "Step two" explains that we must come to realize a power greater than ourselves can and will restore us to sanity if we are willing to seek God's help. The alcoholic must not turn to other drugs—street drugs, or prescription drugs like pain killers or tranquilizers—for all we are doing is replacing one drug for another and usually ends with us returning to our addiction or consumption, and death. This is the realization that only a power greater than, and outside of our own quick fixes, can restore us to sanity.

In my opinion any self-help group or professional doctor or psychiatrist who does not prescribe faith and help from the higher power God is only a temporary solution, like a band aid on a shotgun wound. We need God to help heal us from the inside out! Naturally, not every medical, psychological, or other scientific expert will see exactly eye to eye with AA or NA programs, and this is okay, for we know that some of these people have not been in our shoes.

They don't comprehend "Step three", where we must turn our will and our very lives over to the care of God. As we understand Him, and do whatever is necessary not to drink or use, we believe AA and NA is the program, with God's help. That makes it possible, if we are willing to work these steps honestly and completely with no half-stepping measures. Many of our old ideas, attitudes, and feelings about drinking or using prove both worthless and maybe self-destructive. We must come to a point where we are willing to throw out our old ways. We must surrender our will over to God and allow Him to guide us in how to live a sober life.

This is my ultimate goal with AA and NA. Their steps and traditions have helped thousands of alcoholics work this 'recovery' program. Going to AA and NA meetings is important. Hitting bottom opened my mind and I became willing to try something different. What I tried was AA and NA. My new life in the fellowship was a little like learning how to ride a bike for the first time. AA and NA became my training wheels and my supporting hand. It's not that I wanted this help so much at the time; I simply did not want to hurt like that again. My desire to avoid hitting bottom again was more powerful than my desire to drink or use. In the beginning that was what kept me sober. But after a while I found myself working the steps to the best of my ability. I soon realized that my attitudes and actions were changing—if ever so slightly. "One day at a time", I became comfortable with myself, and others, and my hurting started to heal. Thank God for the training wheels and supporting hand that I choose to call Alcoholics Anonymous and Narcotics Anonymous.

Get Help

by Louis

Based on my experiences before and in prison, the best that I can share is to suggest "get help." Get help from the best qualified people and groups.

I believe a majority of prisoners have been traumatized in life. I've listened to histories of being abused as children and exposed to violence as young adults, such that violence has led to their personalities being affected to be constantly angry, frustrated, anxious, and paranoid! Being imprisoned exposes a person to witnessing violence and perhaps being a victim of violence. My siblings and I were repeatedly abandoned, beaten, abused, and molested as children. All three of us grew into self-medicating alcoholics and rage-aholics. These are symptoms of post-traumatic stress.

I could never fit in as a teenager or adult with successful, mature, and sober people. I instinctively sought out my own alcohol-dependent, spiritually damaged kind. I never addressed the root causes of my job failures and inappropriate violent emotions.

When I was 27 years old, I murdered a stranger I had met for the first time. The events of that crime I shall spare.

What I will share is that if I had addressed the post-traumatic stress issues in therapy when I was younger, the murder would not have occurred.

So, here we are in prison, and it's time to get help for issues we need to clean up. To have a good life from here on out.

Alcoholics Anonymous and Narcotics Anonymous work —and Al-Anon—to help me deal with my alcoholic parents.

Triple CMS offers PTS group therapy and one-on-one therapy. Psychiatric drugs are not mandatory. I never take them.

Outside volunteers may offer PTSD recovery groups as well. Groups that address anger issues, domestic violence issues, and conflict resolution methods exist.

I've taken all of them and over the years they have all come together as a whole, knitted threads into the fabric of a new me – including the me I was before the abuse started when I was five years old.

I have peace, sobriety, and social and communication skills, which have elevated my being, to a plateau of enlightenment, delight, and serenity.

Take care of yourself. Get help.

III. FOR INCARCERATED VETERANS

The Veterans Service Office Service Center

by Richard Ranta, Chairman, Veterans Services, CTF Prison

This *Survival Book* is in memory of both Ed Munis and Michael "Doc" Piper. Mr. Munis passed away on August 8, 2018, two weeks after receiving a parole date from the Board of Prison Hearings. Mr. Piper passed away on March 17, 2019. He was awaiting a resentencing hearing at Duel Vocational Institution, when he passed away.

They were an inspiration to everyone, both veterans and non- veterans. They did all they could to help everyone. They also brought educational / self-help programs to the line and continued to do so until their deaths. Their impact for helping inmates will never be forgotten because of this book.

Life in prison can be pretty senseless, chaotic, or even out of hand. It wasn't until I met Doc for the second time, when I first arrived here at Correctional Training Facility that I truly felt like a veteran. I had met Doc when I was at CSP-Solano back around the year 2000. It was only in passing, as he and another inmate were trying to get a Veterans group started there. I was behind them in their endeavors. After Doc left there, I pretty much forgot about him, as we do with most of the relationships we have in prison. I started helping get that Veterans group started. It finally got off the ground around 2006 and was still running when I left there in 2009.

When I got to CTF I was housed in the same wing as Doc and Ed. Ed and Doc co-founded the CTF-Veterans Service Office Service Center. They were both Vietnam combat veterans. When I first came into the wing, Doc came up to me and asked me if I was a Veteran. I told him I was. The next question took me by surprise. He asked me if I had any injuries from my service time. I had never been asked that before by anyone. I didn't think I had, but before I started to answer him, I remembered that I had indeed injured my back twice in the service. He told me to stop by his office when I got off of RTQ (Restricted to Quarters) status. The next day he was at my cell door with some forms for me to fill out, saying that we should get the paperwork going now instead of waiting until I got off RTQ status.

At first I was a little unsure about filling out any paperwork for an inmate who I really didn't know that well. He kept assuring me that I had benefits that were due to me from those injuries. When I got off RTQ, I went to his office. It was this little storage closet that he and his cofounder, had made into an office, except it was like no office that I'd ever seen. The room had space for maybe one little person to fit in it, because of the computers and file cabinets that were in there. He went over the forms with me and told me that I would be interviewed by someone who worked for the County Veterans Service Office.

I had my interview, and, over the years, Doc continued the fight for my VA benefits. He made sure that I wouldn't give up on it, and, that one day, I would receive those benefits. I had my hip replaced in 2017 and needed to find a different job, one that wouldn't require too much manual labor on my part. I talked to Ed and Doc about coming to work in their office. I had seen what they had accomplished and wanted to be a part of that. After Ed was transferred to another prison, I kept showing up to the office to help Doc in any way I could. I knew he was handling a huge job all by himself and I knew he needed the help. Doc was not one that asked for help. He would try to do it alone and that was my way of giving back to him for all he had done for me. Ed passed away in August 2018. Doc put together a Memorial service for him in the Chapel here. There was a new bill that passed in the State, that allowed Veterans with certain injuries be allowed to go back to court for resentencing. Doc and I filed for it. Doc went out to court for resentencing in March of 2019. He was awaiting his hearing at another prison that was close to the County where he was sentenced. They found him unresponsive a few days later. He never made it to court. Both of them will be missed terribly by everyone here at CTF and all the prisons where they had claimants. Those claimants are at most of California's prisons and 28 other State and Federal prisons.

They have helped recover close to $21 million for veterans and their families. Almost $19 million of that amount has gone to the spouses, parents, and children of those incarcerated veterans.

This book is dedicated to those two incarcerated veterans who took an idea and overcame many obstacles, to start something that has spread throughout this great country of ours. Their selfless act of giving back to others, has spread to many other inmates here and throughout the U.S. Their legacy will continue on. Their goal of helping every incarcerated veteran is contagious. It took me within its grasp and has brought me into the office to continue on the work they started. They were incarcerated veterans but they should be remembered as heroes, because of the work they have done. Leave no one behind is something they were taught in the military, they believed it and it showed in the work they did, as was the motto of the office which is:

"HELPING OURSELVES BY HELPING OTHERS"

Rough, Tough Ready for Anything, Is PTSD REAL?

by Michael 'Doc' Piper

I am writing to all of you that have served in a theater of combat or maybe you just think that you are alone and crazy and that behavior such as beating on your spouse, drinking heavily, doing drugs either by prescription or not, to self-medicate is acceptable behavior, think again.

Seeking help is not a sign of weakness nor is talking about it. Far too many men and women serving in combat zones or in stressful environments fail to understand the seriousness of their behavior.

Too many men and women are occupying unnecessary space in prison throughout the United States. By one estimate, there are approximately 200 thousand veterans incarcerated in State and Federal Prisons. What does this mean, well I would say, be very careful how you carry yourself, seek help, recognize that the John Wayne mentality does no one any good.

You depend on your comrade in combat without question, he has your back and you have his.

Well let's take that a step further, never stop looking out. You will never in your lifetime experience the type of camaraderie or personal pain as that you will experience in combat.

Know it understand it, learn from it. It can help you grow both as a person and a productive part of our society. Decide now, not later save everyone you love the heartbreak that may follow.

What should you do? The only advice I can provide is seek professional counseling. I am not advocating telling your command that you have problems or go to the Chaplin for advice. I served in Vietnam and prayer was not the answer I was looking for. I became part of an early PTSD group offered when the VA actually told us "we had no problems."

We knew better, drinking, drugs raising all kinds of hell, living on the edge, the rush, feeling alone, crazy, abusing our spouse, friends, family. It doesn't take long before you build up some sort of police record, then what! The abuse to yourself and others turns into a life sentence. Once again bye, bye World!

If you are on active duty, you might seek outside counseling by a trained professional, work through your doubt, your anger; your 'what the hell is really going on?' If you are discharged, even if you have an other-than-honorable discharge, the VA has an obligation to provide you the assistance you are entitled. Go to the VA, look up a Veterans Outreach Center, get that help and file a claim for service-connected benefits, once again, you are entitled!

Stay out of my prison; I have enough problems going on than to listen to you because you got stupid. Prison is not the place to find yourself; nothing going on here, no redeeming social values here. You decide, there is no one else to blame.

An incarcerated veteran, and different kind of lifer.

Originally written for Survival Guide 2017.

(Untitled)

by Chris Pesqueira

This is the real deal, dude. All that Hollywood crap you think you know about doing time, get that shit out of your head. Prison today is not what it used to be, but in prison, the old ways are still the best ways.

To extend your time in prison, that is. How do I know, you ask? I have now been incarcerated for over 32 years on a 15 to life sentence for 2nd degree murder. I know a thing or two about stepping on my own dick.

Daily survival is easy—be yourself, not who you think you need to appear to be. You, my brother, are a veteran. You freely chose to serve your country, with a set of morals and values that will carry you through this time in your life.

Okay, so you fucked up. Why did you fuck up? Own it, reflect on it, and what led up to it.

DO NOT DENY IT!

You are responsible for you; and allowing some dude you've never met to dictate how you will do your time, is not something you want to get into. Just like going into the service and raising your own hand to take the oath,

You were the only one in that set of handcuffs when you got busted. Now is not the time to entertain any thoughts of entering the realm of "Prison Politics".

You already belong to an honorable brotherhood, so seek out fellow veterans. You'll be quite surprised at just how much we all have in common regardless of cultural, religious or geographical differences. We're all green inside, we're family and we truly understand one another when no one else can.

One of my greatest mistakes was having an ego and pride so overblown that I truly believed I had everything under control at all times. BULLSHIT!

Mistake two, being so full of bravado that I didn't seek out personnel that could assist me in a greater understanding of how I could be solely responsible for the committing of a murder in cold blood that was in no way necessary. Living in denial only led to a self-hatred and loss of self-esteem, and that led to drug abuse and involvement with Prison Politics.

My moral compass was in disarray. Loss of hope was right there to further my continued drug use, leading to addiction, and all the furthering of pain, shame, guilt that comes with it.

"What the fuck has this got to do with me?", you ask. Well, dude, it's actually pretty simple, do you remember K.I.S.S.? (Keep It Simple, Stupid). It's my message to you. What I've gone through, you do not have to repeat.

If you haven't completed your education, do so. Do you have prior alcohol/substance abuse? Seek self-help, possibly S.A.P.—substance abuse program. Learn about spousal/domestic violence. Check out Alternatives to Violence project (AVP).

There is help and it is not a weakness to seek help. It takes courage, integrity, and a desire to better oneself.

Oh shit! Doesn't that sound like a veteran? Do I sound like some motivational speaker or mentor of some sort? That's crazy!

I'm an Airborne Ranger, 1/75th. HOOAH! I'll always lead the way.

{Mr. Pesqueira was recently found suitable for parole}.

A Survivor's Guide for Incarcerated Veterans

by Edwin V. Munis, former Chairman, Veterans Service Office

In 2004, Edwin V. Munis K59703 and Michael D. "Doc" Piper J49677 developed and implemented the Correctional Training Facility Veterans Service Office Service Center in Soledad, California. The CTF-VSO remains the only fully functional Veterans Service Office in compliance with Public Law 107-95 (2001) in any prison— state or federal— in the United States dedicated to the incarcerated veterans and their families.

Munis and Piper are both incarcerated at the Correctional Training Facility, Soledad California; both served in highly decorated combat units in Vietnam from 1966 through 1968. Ed served with the 25th Infantry Division HHC 2nd BDE, and the 2/27 Infantry Regiment "Wolfhounds" as an RTO, he is currently 100% service connected for his service in Vietnam by the United States

Department of Veterans Affairs

"Doc" served in the U.S. Navy with the 1st and 3rd Marine Force Recon Units as a Corpsman, he is currently 80% service connected by the VA and both are receiving compensation monthly from the VA. From the Ho Bo Woods in III Corps to the Siege of Khe Sanh in I Corps, they continue to serve their fellow veteran where ever they may be.

None of this would have been possible without the full support of former Wardens A.P. Kane, Ben Curry, Randy Grounds and current Warden Marion Spearman. Correctional Lieutenant Eric Darosa has been supervising Munis and Piper in this endeavor from 2005 until 2017.

The CTF-VSO has been fortunate to have had the support of Correctional Officers and free staff alike— a fragile existence relying on openness and serving a common cause. Since 2010 when the CTF-VSO filed for direct accreditation with the Veterans Administration the VA has offered continual resistance to their recognition and plight of the incarcerated veteran. We will continue the offensive. VA/VC same/same, from one hostile environment to another, the fight for veteran recognition continues.

Know that once you pass the initial bureaucratic bumbling of the VA, you will enter the best health care system in the United States second to none.

A Survivors Guide For Incarcerated Veterans: Introduction

From the military to prison, if you survived your military service you can survive prison. If you failed in the military it can't be said that you will fail in prison, there are some who actually thrive in the prison environment.

This guide is written to let you know that incarceration does not mean you will lose your VA benefits; you still retain certain rights with certain exceptions, such as a Court Martial, that alone, is a Bar to benefits. Honorable or general under honorable conditions entitles the holder to most all benefits available with some limitations on education. Under other than honorable conditions will be entirely dependent on the United States Department of Veterans' Affairs with consideration given your specific circumstances.

You can always file to the Board for Correction of Military Records for an update or review in discharge characterization. The Board does not have the final say so with what the VA may or may not find you eligible for, the Board can determine an injustice in your specific instance, and possibly, upgrade your discharge to under honorable conditions.

This guide is not intended to be an answer to all your questions it is simply a guide, the actual research and follow up is your responsibility

Prison like anything else is a matter of attitude, if you want attention brought to yourself you will have all the attention you desire and in most cases more than you want to deal with. It is not unusual for a prison term of ten

(10) years to turn into a life sentence. This is unfortunately not that uncommon; everyday somewhere in the system someone is adding a life sentence to an already existing term, or continually being denied a parole.

The purpose of obtaining your VA entitlements is to provide you with some level of comfort. Your documented in-service injuries are compensable, including injuries that take place while you are on leave, as long as it is not characterized as willful misconduct.

You have available while incarcerated a means to obtain a higher education and develop skills to aid with your parole suitability. For those that get granted a 30% or higher disability rating from

VA, a chance to help your family's financial needs or your children's education assistance is conceivable. What an opportunity.

There are options, just know they are available. Don't lose your VA entitlements just because you are pissed off. We are all pissed off! Some of us handle it a little better than others. The shit will always be the shit and it will never smell like roses. You survived before and you can do it again. An important FACT, a common misconception that less-than honorable discharges are upgraded to honorable after six months is untrue. This supposed fact often times was used to move you along. Your only entitlement is to file an appeal with the Board for Correction of Military Records.

VA Entitlements and Incarceration
Title 38 U.S. Code Service, Code of Federal Regulations. The Law!

When Congress enacted Title 38 (United States Code Service and the Code of Federal Regulations) incarcerated veterans were included. Depending on the character of your discharge you are no less entitled to your benefits than any other veteran that honorably served our Nation.

This includes compensation for injuries received while on active duty. (Title 38 C.F.R. § 3.665, Incarcerated Beneficiaries and Fugitive Felons' Compensation.)

The amount of compensation an incarcerated veteran may receive is limited by regulation. You can receive no more than the amount received by a veteran receiving the amount that equals a 10% rating. That means if your service connection is rated at 20% or higher, the maximum amount you may receive during incarceration—considering today's rating structure—will be $130.94 monthly. If your rating is at the 10% level then your entitlement by regulation will be half the 10% amount or $65.00. If your rating is 30% or greater your dependents may become eligible to receive the balance of your compensation by your requesting an apportionment of benefit, directed to your eligible dependents, this includes in some circumstances your parents, VA form 21-0788. An additional dependent allowance is provided to veterans that have eligible dependents. The VA will provide the necessary forms with instructions and assistance to complete this process.

You as an incarcerated veteran are "entitled" to file a claim for service connection just as any other veteran, VA form 21-526EZ. This can be done by representing yourself or having an accredited organization represent you. You should provide a copy of your DD-214 when you submit your application; your claim will not be processed without the DD214, this helps the VA move your paper work along. Court Martial and some Other Than Honorable Discharges will disqualify your application. If you are an Other-Than-Honorable (OTH) the VA has the sole authority to grant your benefits depending on the nature and circumstances involved. If you received an OTH by negotiating to avoid a Court Martial your military records will show this to be the case and your claim will be denied. A Court Martial is an automatic Bar to VA benefits.

Step by step: Use a Standard form 180 to request your DD214, military records, including the administrative and medical records contained in your file. Mail the completed form or request a form from the National Personnel Records Center, (Military Personnel Records) 1 Archives Drive St. Louis, MO. 63138-1002. If you have an idea when and where you were injured, so state, this will help to locate the records required to substantiate your claim.

The VA has a duty to assist all veterans when filing a plausible claim (VA's Duty to Assist, Title 38 United States Code §5107(a)). Gather your personal medical records from your private physician, if you were receiving treatment from a private provider prior to your incarceration. If you are incarcerated request copies of your medical records from the infirmary at your particular institution, there may be a charge for this service. If you are indigent you should have no problem. When visiting the infirmary, be sure to mention that your injury was incurred while you were on active duty, your treating physician, in most situations is obligated to make this entry and it will later assist with establishing your Nexus Statement. The link between your military service and your continued need for treatment, this is very critical to your claim. Active duty service includes any injuries received while you were on leave or a pass, be sure you know where to locate these records. Although the VA has a duty to assist this does not include inquiring from any possible source, you must be able to identify where your records may be, County Hospital or Clinic, Military Installation, this is your responsibility, the VA is required by law to obtain any records in the custody of a federal agency applicable to your claim.

If VA determines your claim is unsupported and denies your claim then file a Notice of Disagreement and ask for a Statement of Case. Just because the VA says no, does not mean that the no is final. Nothing is final until you have been provided the opportunity to make full use of the appeals process, which includes the Board of Veterans Appeals VA form VA9 (BVA) and the U.S. Court of Appeals for Veterans Claims, (USCVA) both are located in Washington DC. If the BVA denies your claim, well once again that does not mean no, you still have the opportunity to file an appeal in the Court, when the Court Dockets your appeal your docket number and name will be posted on a roster available to Attorney's and Accredited Practitioners, you very well may be contacted by a Firm or Agency specializing in Veterans Claims. Once you receive an answer to your Notice of Disagreement along with your Statement of Case you will be under some very specific time lines, example NOD with SOC you have 60 days to reply, then when you hear from the regional office on your SOC you will have 30 days to return your appeal to the Board of Veterans appeals (VA-9) if any of these deadlines are missed your claim will be denied and you will lose your filing date (retroactive date of claim). A new claim must be filed with new and material evidence, meaning medical documentation. The Board will refer your claim back for remand to the Regional Office, if the Board holds to the Regional Office position you have 30 days to file an appeal to the United States Court of Appeals for Veterans Claims. It is at this level of appeal you may retain counsel for representation. Do Not Sit on any paperwork thinking you have time to respond, fact is you have no time. You are in prison and as far out of the loop as a claimant can be, it's on you the Veteran to follow through.

When you are contacted by a Firm or Agency you will be asked to provide some information regarding your claim. The Court is required to post the BVA decision, in a nationwide directory. You will not be charged for this consultation; regulations provide for attorney fees to be paid from a special program. There may come a point in your Attorney/Client relationship, regarding your claim that fees are appropriate, in that instant the fee generally does not exceed 20%, based on contingency.

In 2005 the Correctional Training Facility in Soledad, California formally established the first fully functional Veterans Service Office Service Center in the U.S. As a demonstration program of referral and counseling for veterans transitioning from certain institutions who are at risk of homelessness which includes prisons. (*Public Law 107-95 (2001.) Title 38 USCS, Benefits for Homeless Veterans. Chapter 20 Subchapter III, Training and Outreach. § 2023*)

The CTF-VSO has assisted in the recovery of over $15 million dollars in service-connected compensation due incarcerated veterans and their dependents; apportionment to dependents exceeds $13 million dollars.

(Editor's note: since Ed wrote this, compensation received with the assistance of the VSO has reached more than $20 million dollars}

The CTF-VSO is currently assisting incarcerated veterans in 35 California Prisons and 35 prisons located in 23 other states, this includes 3 federal facilities, and the Department of Army Disciplinary Barracks Fort Leavenworth. The CTF-VSO is certified by the Monterey County Office of Military and Veterans Affairs, pending direct Accreditation by the U.S. Department of Veterans Affairs, Counsel General and V.A. Secretary. The CTF-VSO is operated and was developed by two incarcerated Vietnam Veterans, presently collecting their exempt from restitution compensation.

Don't forfeit your benefits because of your incarceration. You and your family deserve all entitlements provided by law. No does not always mean no, especially when the VA says no.

Denial of Claim for Failure to Appear

It is not uncommon for the VA to deny an incarcerated veteran claim due to the veteran's inability to appear for a scheduled VA Compensation and Pension examination, this type of examination will only be requested by the VA if you have presented a plausible claim, meaning something is there. If your claim is denied for this reason, immediately file a Notice of Disagreement and remind the VA of its Duty to Assist. Incarcerated veterans by citing Title 38 United States Code § 5107(a). If this is the case, **simply state:**

"I recently received the VA denial of my claim. In the denial it was noted that the veteran failed to appear for a scheduled examination. Once again remind the VA that I am incarcerated and as such will be unable to attend." "See Bolton v. Brown, 8 Vet. App. at 191. (1995.) Wood v. Derwinski, 1 Vet. App. 190, 193 (1991).

The duty to assist incarcerated veterans requires the VA to tailor its assistance to meet the peculiar circumstances of confinement; as such individuals are "entitled" to the same care and consideration given their fellow veterans. Wood v. Derwinski, 1 Vet. App. 190, 193 (1991); Bolton v. Brown, 8 Vet. App. 185, 191 (1995).

VA does not have the authority to require a correctional institution to release a Veteran so that VA can provide him/her the necessary examination at the closest VA medical facility. See e.g., 38 U.S.C.A. Section 5711. Nevertheless, VA's duty to assist an incarcerated Veteran includes:

(1) attempting to arrange transportation of the claimant to a VA facility for examination;

(2) contacting the correctional facility and having their medical

personnel conduct the examination according to VA examination worksheets; or

(3) sending a VA or Fee base examiner to the correctional facility to conduct the examination. See Bolton v. Brown, 8 Vet. App. At 191.

'The Court has cautioned those who adjudicate claims of incarcerated veterans to be certain that they tailor their assistance to the peculiar circumstances of confinement. Such individuals are entitled to the same care and consideration given to their fellow veterans. (Bolton.).'

Please provide me with a Statement of Case (SOC) so I may proceed. "

If available, use VA form 21-4138, Statement in Support of Claim. If none are available make your remarks on a standard 8 ½ x 11 sheet of paper, this is acceptable and will hold up in court as proper notice.

The VA Adjudication Procedures Manual contains a provision for scheduling examinations of incarcerated veterans. The Manual calls for the AOJ or local Veterans Health Administration (VHA) Medical Examination Coordinator to confer with prison authorities to determine whether the Veteran should be escorted to a VA facility for examination by VHA personnel. If that is not possible the Veteran may be examined at the prison by:

(1) VHA personnel;

(2) prison medical providers at VA EXPENSE; or

(3) fee-based providers contracted by VA. See M21-1MR, Part III. Iv. 3. A. II. D.

When a claimant fails to report for an examination scheduled in conjunction with the original compensation claim, the claim may be rated on the evidence or record. Title 38 C.F.R., Section 3.665 (b). When the medical evidence is inadequate, the VA must supplement the record by seeking an advisory opinion or ordering another medical examination. Colvin v. Derwinski, 1 Vet. App. 171 (1991) and Hatlestad v. Derwinski, 3 Vet. App.

213 (1993). Again, no does not mean no! Be persistent. The VA does not have the final word, that happens only when you give up.

VA Entitlements and Incarceration
Hiring an Attorney to Represent You

If you filed a Notice of Disagreement with VA after June 20, 2007 and believe you were denied unjustly or if in your opinion the claims examiner made an error you may need the counsel of an attorney. Poor rating decisions by VA Rating officers are unfortunately not all that uncommon, The VA is seriously lacking the ability to keep up with the claims review process and coupled with poor training will only lead to longer delays with the adjudication of your claim. File a new claim VA form 21-526EZ; present all new medical evidence supporting your injury(s) from institutional or private physicians.

Traditionally, attorneys were barred from representing veterans until after a decision was rendered by the Board of Veterans Appeals (BVA) and the case went to the Veterans Court.

Prior to the change in regulation your only option was to seek claims assistance from an accredited veteran's organization or your counties veteran's service office. (VSO)

With the change in law, veterans and their families now have the option of hiring an attorney to represent them with their claims, in addition to the services of a County Veterans Service Office or Veterans Service Organization. There are some situations where hiring an attorney may be an advantage other than to going with the County Service Officer or a Veterans Service

Organization. Attorneys are required to carefully examine the merits of a claim and limit their case load to only the number of cases they can handle, while County Service Offices or Veteran Service Organizations do not limit nor are they required to limit their case load. I have never known of a County Veterans Service Office file claims purely for the sake of doing so.

In California we are fortunate to have a strong State Association of County Veteran Service Officers; they are responsible for the development of a plausible claim, one that has merit. Not all states have Veterans Service Offices. Unfortunately, one shortcoming is some service officers are prejudiced because of your incarceration; never forget that you are not any less entitled to your benefits than any other honorably discharged veteran. See Title 38 Code of Federal Regulations section 3.665, the law is clear.

The Veterans Court does not award benefits, the Court corrects errors by overturning a BVA ruling on a factual point or procedural error. The Board is required to follow the guidelines issued by the Court.

An attorney practicing before the Court can save you time, frustration and aggravation by assisting you and your family, and help speed you on to a favorable decision once the Court has remanded your claim back to be revaluated by BVA. The Court has been reluctant to reverse many cases deferring to the Board's fact-finding powers; it is more common for the Court to remand your claim back to BVA

An order remanding your case back to the BVA requires that the Board issue a new decision. This is important because it allows a veteran or dependent to submit any additional evidence or argument to win the claim. The Court also corrects the Boards misapplication of the law. This is a second chance to win your benefits and protect your original filing date. The filing date is the date used to determine how much the VA must pay in retroactive benefits if an award is made. Be aware that many attorneys do not represent your case once remanded to the Board; ask your attorney if your representation will continue, many attorneys will continue to represent you on contingency. The government pays attorney fees for representation at the Court, under the Equal Access to Justice Act (EAJA), on an issue of remand it is common and within the law for an attorney to charge you a contingency fee, most often no more than 20 percent of any past due (retroactive) benefits awarded.

If anyone would like a listing of attorneys practicing before the U.S. Court of Veterans Appeals for Veterans Claims, you may contact:

Clerk of the Court
625 Indiana Avenue, N.W.

Suite 900
Washington, DC. 2004
(202) 501-5470

U.S. Department of Veterans Affairs (VBA)
810 Vermont Ave. N.W.
Washington, D.C. 20420

For information or assistance from the CTF VSO you may contact:
Captain Michael Deverick
CTF-VSO Supervisor
Correctional Training Facility
Veterans Service Office Service Center
P.O. Box 705
Soledad, California 93960-0705

Incarceration PTSD and In-Service Injuries

It is estimated by the Department of Justice, Bureau of Statics, that there are approximately 180,000 incarcerated veterans in U.S. Prisons today {2017}. California alone has 17,000 incarcerated veterans throughout the correctional system.

One of the concerns a veteran may have when entering prison, is the availability of medical and mental health services. The Departments of Corrections are not known for their quality of medical care on any level. This often leaves incarcerated veterans' the task of developing their own resources'. This can be accomplished with the help of various inmate activity groups that are active in many prisons. You might look into the possibility of joining a veteran's group: Often times this is a good place to find the comradeship you once experienced during your active military service, including a safe place to vent your frustrations.

Prison has different levels of security, from your Super Max to your fire camps. Racism is a fact of life and you must be careful how you carry yourself.

Most serious injuries and even death are due to the invisible lines that exist in prison. Pay attention, ask questions within your own peer group, but while doing so remember they don't always have the answers either. Pay attention. If you are a combat veteran and experiencing problems, the mental health care services at your institution may have a means to sign up to see a psychologist for help and referral for medications if that is an avenue that may be helpful. Groups can be helpful. Remember to honor your service. War stories can and will be sorted out, if you are one of those comic book war heroes, you will be found, out, and from the more serious veterans' you tell about sustaining injury because of your inventiveness and tendency to exacerbate the facts surrounding your specific time in the military. There is always someone who served in a super-duper secret operations branch, like "I served in black ops, they were so secret, I can't discuss it." Be careful and above all be honest, don't live in your shadow, you are doing no one any good mostly yourself. Get help.

If you have a sound basis to file a 'well-grounded claim' with the VA for PTSD, then by all means do so. Request by using the form 180 to get all of your in-service medical records. This will be very helpful with developing your Nexis, between your service and your continued need for treatment. Tell your psychologist that you believe your behavior is linked to your combat experiences. Your military records will tell a clearer story, by supporting your claim, or by leaving you standing without any basis to establish service connection.

Let's suppose you suffered a physical injury while on duty. May be during training with pugil sticks during close quarters combat training, or while you were playing baseball and slid into third base. If you went to the base infirmary for any injuries whatsoever and reported it, this is the type of medical reports you are looking for. A weekend pass or leave back home, you were still on active duty and these injuries may be compensable. If you were out drinking with your buddies and you fell on your ass and cracked your head requiring hospitalization for concussion, you just screwed up an otherwise good claim by committing what the VA calls "willful misconduct."

When you visit the treating physician at the prison infirmary, relate your injuries to this type of activity. Combat injuries are a little clearer, although I have seen shrapnel wounds characterized as "not combat related." Tell the medical examiner I was injured doing this or that activity, relate it to your service. Scars are compensable, have that noted. Exposures to certain chemicals are compensable if you were exposed to burn pits while serving in Iraq or Afghanistan. Chemicals while serving on the flight deck of an aircraft carrier, or solvents in the engine room, dust from brake pads, these are sure signs exposure to asbestosis. This type of exposure must be considered when filing a claim with the VA, overlook nothing, so many of us forget about what we did while serving and it's these little things that are so important in the claims process.

DSM-V Diagnostic Criteria for PTSD

by Veterans Affairs National Center for PTSD

(Editor's note: Ed's original writing on the criteria for DSM-IV has been replaced by diagnostic criteria listed in the more recent DSM V, as described on the Department of Veterans Affairs National Center for PTSD website}.

PTSD and DSM-5

In 2013, the American Psychiatric Association revised the PTSD diagnostic criteria in the fifth edition of its Diagnostic and Statistical Manual of Mental Disorders (DSM-5; 1). PTSD is included in a new category in DSM-5, Trauma- and Stressor-Related Disorders. All of the conditions included in this classification require exposure to a traumatic or stressful event as a diagnostic criterion. For a review of the DSM-5 changes to the criteria for PTSD, see the American Psychiatric Association website on Posttraumatic Stress Disorder.

DSM-5 Criteria for PTSD

Full copyrighted criteria are available from the American Psychiatric Association. All of the criteria are required for the diagnosis of PTSD. The following text summarizes the diagnostic criteria:

Criterion A (one required): The person was exposed to: death, threatened death, actual or threatened serious injury, or actual or threatened sexual violence, in the following way(s):

Direct exposure
- Witnessing the trauma
- Learning that a relative or close friend was exposed to a trauma
- Indirect exposure to aversive details of the trauma, usually in the course of professional duties (e.g., first responders, medics)

Criterion B (one required): The traumatic event is persistently re-experienced, in the following way(s):
- Unwanted upsetting memories
- Nightmares
- Flashbacks
- Emotional distress after exposure to traumatic reminders
- Physical reactivity after exposure to traumatic reminders

Criterion C (one required): Avoidance of trauma-related stimuli after the trauma, in the following way(s):
- Trauma-related thoughts or feelings
- Trauma-related reminders

Criterion D (two required): Negative thoughts or feelings that began or worsened after the trauma, in the following way(s):
- Inability to recall key features of the trauma
- Overly negative thoughts and assumptions about oneself or the world
- Exaggerated blame of self or others for causing the trauma
- Negative affect
- Decreased interest in activities
- Feeling isolated
- Difficulty experiencing positive affect

Criterion E (two required): Trauma-related arousal and reactivity that began or worsened after the trauma, in the following way(s):
- Irritability or aggression

- Risky or destructive behavior
- Hypervigilance
- Heightened startle reaction
- Difficulty concentrating
- Difficulty sleeping

Criterion F (required): Symptoms last for more than 1 month.

Criterion G (required): Symptoms create distress or functional impairment (e.g., social, occupational).

Criterion H (required): Symptoms are not due to medication, substance use, or other illness.

Two specifications:

- **Dissociative Specification.** In addition to meeting criteria for diagnosis, an individual experiences high levels of either of the following in reaction to trauma-related stimuli:
- **Depersonalization.** Experience of being an outside observer of or detached from oneself (e.g., feeling as if "this is not happening to me" or one were in a dream).
- **Derealization.** Experience of unreality, distance, or distortion (e.g., "things are not real").
- **Delayed Specification.** Full diagnostic criteria are not met until at least six months after the trauma(s), although onset of symptoms may occur immediately.

(Note: DSM-5 introduced a preschool subtype of PTSD for children ages six years and younger.)

How Do the DSM-5 PTSD Symptoms Compare to DSM-IV Symptoms?

Overall, the symptoms of PTSD are generally comparable between DSM-5 and DSM-IV. A few key alterations include:

The revision of Criterion A1 in DSM-5 narrowed qualifying traumatic events such that the unexpected death of family or a close friend due to natural causes is no longer included.

Criterion A2, requiring that the response to a traumatic event involved intense fear, hopelessness, or horror, was removed from DSM-5. Research suggests that Criterion A2 did not improve diagnostic accuracy (2).

The avoidance and numbing cluster (Criterion C) in DSM-IV was separated into two criteria in DSM-5: Criterion C (avoidance) and Criterion D (negative alterations in cognitions and mood). This results in a requirement that a PTSD diagnosis includes at least one avoidance symptom. Three new symptoms were added:

Criterion D (Negative thoughts or feelings that began or worsened after the trauma): Overly negative thoughts and assumptions about oneself or the world; and, negative affect

Criterion E (Trauma-related arousal and reactivity that began or worsened after the trauma): Reckless or destructive behavior

A. The person has been exposed to a traumatic event in which both the following were present:

(1) The person experienced, witnessed, or was confronted with an event or event involved actual or threatened death or serious injury, or a threat to physical integrity of self or others.

(2) The persons' response involved intense fear, helplessness, or horror.

B. The traumatic event is persistently re-experienced in one (or more) of the following ways:

(1) Recurrent and intrusive distressing recollections of the event, including images, thoughts, or perceptions.

(2) Recurrent distressing dreams of the event.

(3) Acting or feeling as if the traumatic event were recurring (includes a sense of reliving the experience, illusions, hallucinations, and dissociative flashback episodes, including those that occur on awakening or when intoxicated.)

(4) Intense psychological distress at exposure to internal or external cues that symbolize or resemble an aspect of the traumatic event.

(5) Psychological reactivity on exposure to internal or external cues that symbolize or resemble an aspect of the traumatic event.

C. Persistent avoidance of stimuli associated with the trauma and numbing of general responsiveness (not present before the trauma,) as indicated by three (or more) of the following:

(1) Efforts to avoid thoughts, feelings, or conversations associated with the trauma.

(2) Efforts to avoid activities, places or people that arouse recollections of the trauma:

(3) Inability to recall an important aspect of the trauma.

(4) Markedly diminished interest or participation in significant activities.

(5) Feeling of detachment or estrangement from others.

(6) Restricted range of affection (e.g., does not expect to have a career, marriage, children, or normal life span.

D. Persistent symptoms of increased arousal (not present before trauma,) as indicated by two (or more) of the following:

(1) Difficulty falling or staying asleep.

(2) Irritability or outbursts of anger.

(3) Difficulty concentrating.

(4) Hyper-vigilance.

(5) Exaggerated startle response.

E. Duration of disturbance (symptoms in Criteria B, C, and D.) is more than once a month

F. The disturbance causes clinically significant distress or impairment in social, occupational, or other important areas of functioning.

Specify if:

- Acute: if duration of symptoms is less than three months.

- Chronic; if duration of symptoms' is three months or more.
- Specify if: With Delayed Onset: If onset of symptoms' is at least six months after the stressor.

List of the Forms Used for Veterans Affairs Benefits

by Veterans Service Office

These are only a few of the many forms the VA uses. As you know, any government entity has many hoops to jump through. Please pay attention to how you fill the forms out and make sure you follow up on anything the VA asks for you to do. Make sure you meet all of their deadlines.

They have a "Duty to Assist", but you will most likely have to do your own legwork on getting your own information.

VA = Veterans Affairs
DD = Department of Defense
NA = National Archives
SF = Standard Form

1. VA Form 10-10EZ Application for Health Benefits (send to VA)

INSTRUCTIONS FOR COMPLETING ENROLLMENT
APPLICATION FOR HEALTH BENEFITS
Please Read Before You Start . . .
What is VA Form 10-10EZ used for?
For Veterans to apply for enrollment in the VA health care system. The information provided on this form will be used by VA to determine your eligibility for medical benefits and on average will take 30 minutes to complete. This includes the time it will take to read instructions, gather the necessary facts and fill out the form.

Where can I get help filling out the form and if I have questions?

You may use ANY of the following to request assistance:

- Ask VA to help you fill out the form by calling us at 1-877-222-VETS (8387).
- Access VA's website at http://www.va.gov and select "Contact the VA."
- Contact the Enrollment Coordinator at your local VA health care facility.
- Contact a National or State Veterans Service Organization.

Definitions of terms used on this form:

SERVICE-CONNECTED (SC): A VA determination that an illness or injury was incurred or aggravated in the line of duty, in the active military, naval or air service.

COMPENSABLE: A VA determination that a service-connected disability is severe enough to warrant monetary compensation. NONCOMPENSABLE: A VA determination that a service-connected disability is not severe enough to warrant monetary compensation.

NONSERVICE-CONNECTED (NSC): A Veteran who does not have a VA determined service-related condition.

2. SF 180 Request Pertaining to Military Records (Standard Form 180 is available online or through authorized Veterans Service Officers; form includes instructions where to send it depending upon the nature of your request)

INSTRUCTION AND INFORMATION SHEET FOR SF 180, REQUEST PERTAINING TO MILITARY

RECORDS 1. General Information. The Standard Form 180, Request Pertaining to Military Records (SF180) is used to request information from military records. Certain identifying information is necessary to determine the location of an individual's record of military service. Please try to answer each item on the SF 180. If you do not have and cannot obtain the information for an item, show "NA," meaning the information is "not available". Include as much of the requested information as you can. Incomplete information may delay response time. To determine where to mail this request see Page 2 of the SF180 for record locations and facility addresses. Online requests may be submitted to the National Personnel Records Center (NPRC) by a veteran or deceased veteran's next-of-kin using eVetRecs at http://www.archives.gov/veterans/military-service-records/ .

3. VA Form 21-22: Appointment of a Veteran's Service Organization as Claimant's Representative
(This form must be submitted to VA if you appoint a veteran's organization to act as your representative)

4. VA Form 21-22a: Appointment of an Individual as Claimant's Representative
(this form must be submitted to VA if you appoint an individual to act as your representative)

5. VA Form 21-0966: Intent to File a Claim for Compensation and/or Pension or Survivors Pension and/or Dependency and Indemnity Compensation (DIC)
(This Form Is Used to Notify VA of Your Intent to File for the General Benefit(s) Checked on the form)

6. VA Form 21-526EZ: Application for Disability and Related Compensation Benefits.
(When to Use this Form: Use this notice and the attached application to submit a claim for veterans'disability compensation and related compensation benefits. This notice informs you of the evidence necessary to decide your claim. After you submit your claim on the attached application you will not receive an initial letter regarding your claim. You do not need to submit another application).

7. VA Form 21-0781: Statement in Support of Claim for Service Connection for Post-Traumatic Stress Disorder (PTSD).

(INSTRUCTIONS: List the stressful incident or incidents that occurred in service that you feel contributed to your current condition. For each incident, provide a description of what happened, the date, the geographic location, your unit assignment and dates of assignment, and the full names and unit assignments of you know of who were killed or injured during the incident. Please provide dates within at least a 60-day range and do not use nicknames. It is important that you complete the form in detail and be as specific as possible so that research of military records can be thoroughly conducted. If more space is needed, attach a separate sheet, indicating the item number to which the answers apply).

8. VA Form 21-0781a: Statement in Support of Claim for Service Connection for Post-Traumatic Stress Disorder (PTSD) Secondary to Personal Assault

(INSTRUCTIONS: same as # 7 above).

9. VA Form 21-0788: Information Regarding Apportionment of Beneficiary's Award.

(INSTRUCTIONS: All or part of a veteran's disability award may be apportioned (paid) to the veteran's spouse, child, or dependent parent. A surviving spouse's award may also be apportioned for the veteran's child or children. Print all answers clearly. If an answer is "none" or "0," write that or line through the space provided. For additional space, attach a separate sheet, indicating the item number to which the answers apply. Make sure to write the veteran's name and VA claim number on any attachments to the form).

10. VA Form 21-4138: Statement in Support of Claim.

INSTRUCTIONS: Read the Privacy Act and Respondent Burden on Page 2 before completing the form. Complete as much of Section I as possible. The information requested will help process your claim for benefits. If you need any additional room, use the second page). SECTION II: REMARKS (The following statement is made in connection with a claim for benefits in the case of the above-named veteran/beneficiary.)

11. VA Form 21-4142: Authorization to Disclose Information to the Department of Veterans Affairs.

(Authorization and consent to release information to va and signature).

12. VA Form 21-4142a: General Release For Medical Provider Information to the Department of Veterans Affairs (VA).

(Authorization and consent to release medical provider information to VA).

13. VA Form 21-4193: Notice to Department of Veterans Affairs of Veteran or Beneficiary Incarcerated in Penal Institution.

(Pursuant to Title 38, U.S.C., 1505, 3482, 3680 and 5313, awards of Department of Veterans Affairs benefits for veterans and beneficiaries are subject to adjustment or discontinuance while such persons are incarcerated. File this form along with your claim to determine any limitations on the specific incarcerated veteran situation you face).

14. VA Form 21P-509: Statement of Dependency of Parent(s).

(Use VA Form 21P-509 if:

You are a veteran whose parents are dependent on you for support, and you are: • Receiving compensation benefits based on a 30 percent or higher service-connected disability, or • Receiving VA educational benefits based on enrollment of 1/2 time or more.

OR

You are the parent of a deceased veteran who: Died on active duty or as a result of service-connected injuries or disease prior to January 1, 1957, or • Died on or after May 1, 1957, and before January 1, 1972, while a waiver of premiums of his/her U.S. Government Life Insurance was in effect).

15. VA Form 3288: Request for and Consent to Release of Information from Individual's Records.

(Required to authorize VA to release information to requested third parties).

16. DD Form 149: Application for Correction of Military Record Under the Provisions of Title 10, U.S. Code, Section 1552.

(Used to request corrections in official military records).

17. DD Form 293: Application for Review of Discharge from the Armed Forces of the United States.

(HOW TO APPY FOR A DISCHARGE UPGRADE—Answer a series of questions to get customized step by step instructions on how to apply for a discharge upgrade or correction. If your application goes through and your discharge is upgraded, you'll be eligible for the VA benefits you earned during your period of service).

18. VA Form VA-9:

(Used to file a notice of disagreement with the Board of Veteran Appeals if you believe your case has not been adjudicated correctly).

19. NA Form 13055:

Request for Information Needed to Reconstruct Medical Data (Used when relevant medical data is not in VA records and further search for records is needed).

20. NA Form 13075:

Questionnaire about Military Service (Used when military records are not located or have been destroyed) All branches of the military consider you to have a strong case for a discharge upgrade if you can show your discharge was connected to any of these categories:

- Mental health conditions, including posttraumatic stress disorder (PTSD)
- Traumatic brain injury (TBI)

- Sexual assault or harassment during military service (at VA, we refer to this as military sexual trauma or MST)
- Sexual orientation (including under the Don't Ask, Don't Tell policy)
  The information you enter on the next page is completely confidential.

Note: If you are filing for an Apportionment, you will need to use the following forms: 21-22; 21-0788; and a 21P-509.

You can contact VA at 1-877-222-VETS (8387) or at their website at: http://www.va.gov and select "Contact the VA". You can access these and any other forms at www.va.gov.vaforms .

Note: The address for the Veterans Service Office Service Center is listed below. You can contact us and we will do all we can to help you through the process. I hope the material in this section, as well as the entire book is helpful to you. Our intent was to inform new inmates to the options they have while incarcerated.

What is the Veterans Service Office of the Correctional Training Facility?

The CTF VSO was established in 2004 by the Administration of Former Warden, A.P. Kane, Associate Director, CDCR, (Ret.) in conjunction with Facility Captain, J.L. Clancy, CDCR, (Ret.). The program was developed and implemented by inmates Ed Munis and M. "Doc" Piper.

The CTF VSO is the first program of this kind in the state of California offering service to the Incarcerated Veteran.

June 22-26, 2011 the VSO in conjunction with the Vietnam Veterans Memorial Foundation also sponsored at no cost a presentation at CTF Prison of "The Wall That Heals".

Purpose of the VSO

To provide advocacy for the incarcerated veteran, and their families, regarding entitlement of Veteran Administration benefits, including entitlement programs from State, County and Federal Agencies.

We Offer the Following Services

- Comprehensive benefit counseling
- V.A. claims preparation and submission
- Claim follow-up
- V.A. claims appeal assistance
- Networking with Federal, State and County Agencies

Information Referral for:

- Employment
- V.A. Medical Care
- Education, including benefits for eligible Dependent Children
- Vocational Training
- Public Assistance
- Transitional Housing

Office Information

As of June 2020, the CTF VSO has relocated to the north yard. Appointments may be scheduled daily.

1830 Hrs. to 1930 Hrs.
By appointment

Current Staff:

Richard Ranta, K61466, BW-116L
CTF Veterans Service Representative
Vietnam Era Veteran, United States Air Force.

CTF VSO V.A. claim supervision and accreditation provided by the Monterey County Office of Military and Veterans Affairs.

VSO Claimants are represented by the California Department of Veterans Affairs and is supported by the California Association of County Veteran Service Officers including the Monterey Board of Supervisors

We Can Assist You with the Following:
- V.A. Compensation (Disability) claims.
- Dependent, Indemnity Compensation aid and assistance.
- V.A. compensation apportionment for eligible spouse, dependent children and dependent parents.
- Vocational Rehabilitation.
- Education Benefits and resources.
- Requests for Military Records and Decorations.
- Discharge Review and Correction of Military Records for Eligible Veterans.
- State Veterans Homes.
- Burial Benefits.
- Pension Benefits Information for the paroling veteran.

Re-Entry contact with the United States Department of Veterans Affairs, Kim Pearson, Reentry Specialist VAMC Palo Alto.

In 2007. CTF VSO started providing assistance to the general inmate population with parole plans, and preparation for the Board of Prison Hearings.

2012 AB2490 Butler established VSO's throughout CDCR. 09/12/2012 by Governor Brown. C. P.C. § 2695, Article 6 Chapter 4, Title 1.

MAIL TO:

Captain Michael Deverick

CTF Veterans Service Office Service Center

CORRECTIONAL TRAINING FACILITY

Highway 101 North, P.O. Box 705

Soledad, CA 93960-0705

Remember… We were all Veterans once, and as such, we proudly and bravely served our country… before we were incarcerated…

The Paradox of PTSD

by Charles Hoge, M.D.

Bridging Gaps in Understanding and Improving Treatment

After a decade of war in Afghanistan and Iraq, it's time to reassess how much progress we've made in addressing the profound impact of post-traumatic stress disorder and other war-related mental health concerns on the lives of veterans and their families. Studies have shown that 5-20 percent of veterans who served in Afghanistan and Iraq meet criteria for PTSD after returning home, with higher rates in personnel who experienced direct combat (those in brigade or regimental combat teams), and lower rates in population samples that include support personnel.

These figures are comparable to those observed in Vietnam veterans.

While PTSD has the most impact, other war-related health concerns also take a toll, especially depression, substance use, and suicide. In addition, large numbers of veterans experience normal readjustment challenges of a milder nature (sometimes referred to as "PTS"). PTSD also has a strong association with physical health problems, such as headaches, back pain, and hypertension.

The experience of coming home from a combat deployment is complex, and the distinction between normal and abnormal transition responses is often unclear. Medical professionals define PTSD based on a specific set of symptoms, which include feeling constantly on edge or hyperalert, having difficulty sleeping, experiencing nightmares, being distracted by intrusive deployment-related memories, feeling a lot of anger, having concentration or memory problems, feeling emotionally numb or detached, or avoiding doing things that were previously enjoyable (such as going out to a crowded mall or movie theater). There may also be feelings of guilt or a strong urge to self-medicate with alcohol or drugs to try to get some sleep or to temporarily forget things that happened downrange.

The paradox is that many of these reactions, which medical professionals label "symptoms", are also necessary adaptive physiological responses in combat and skills that professional warriors hone in their training. There is a naïve expectation in society that veterans should be able to transition home smoothly and lead a 'normal' life after serving in a war zone, with little war-zone experiences. Combat-related responses don't just shut off upon returning home. The body doesn't have an "on-off" switch, for good reasons, since these responses have to do with survival.

PTSD in professional warriors is a paradox that makes it very different from the experiences of civilian victims of trauma—something that is not well appreciated even by many professionals in the mental health field. (There are also parallels between service members and first responders such as police or firefighters). Military personnel train for and expect to encounter combat events, and respond collectively as a team according to their training. Reactions that mental health professionals label 'symptoms'' upon return home are based on adaptive beneficial responses acquired through training and experience working in a war zone. For example, situational awareness where a warrior is alert to environmental cues that might signal an enemy threat is life-saving in combat, but might be labeled as 'hypervigilance' back home. Rigorous mission rehearsal and attention to detail (involving checking and rechecking everything mission related) contributes to 're-experiencing' symptoms, intolerance of mistakes, or should've would've-could've type thinking back home.

Continuous night-time operations and the ability to function on limited sleep causes biological changes in the normal sleep-wake (circadian) cycles that can interfere with sleep after returning home. The ability to direct anger, which helps control fear and shut down pain awareness, makes it more likely for anger and rage to be expressed back home. The ability to shut down other emotion to focus on the mission, even after serious casualties, is an absolutely essential skill in the combat environment, but can turn into numbing and avoidance after deployment. The bottom line is that 'symptoms' are also skills.

The thing that distinguishes PTSD from normal, necessary, and adaptive responses and skills of a combat veteran is the degree to which these reactions interfere with the veteran's ability to make a successful transition home. Generally, if these reactions interfere on an ongoing basis with the ability to enjoy life, have meaningful relationships, or be productive in work, studies, or hobbies, then it's more likely that a medical professional will consider them symptoms of PTSD.

Veterans of the wars in Iraq and Afghanistan have been offered extensive programs to help them in transitioning home, programs that were not available during prior wars. They include routine screening for PTSD and mild traumatic brain injury (mTBI), improved mental health professional services, and education efforts focused on reducing stigma and enhancing resilience. PTSD was not recognized at the time of the Vietnam War, and the last 10-20 years have seen a sharp increase in the availability of evidence-based treatments (those established through rigorous clinical studies).

However, despite all these efforts, outcome data suggest that not nearly enough progress has been made, given the level of attention, resources, and services being directed toward this important problem over many years. Half of veterans in need of mental health care still don't receive services. Among those who do begin treatment, a large percentage drop out before completing a sufficient number of sessions to derive meaningful benefits. It has been estimated that only approximately 20 percent of veterans in need of care receive adequate mental health treatment. The reluctance to seek help spans generations of warriors, not just those of the most recent conflicts.

The Reluctance to Seek Help

The reasons for this include barriers, such as the limited availability of appointments in some facilities, transportation problems, or work or child-care responsibilities interfering with regularly scheduled appointments. There is also stigma, defined as concerns about how one might be viewed by others (such as peers or supervisors) if treatment is sought. Then there are factors that lie within the responsibility of mental health professionals themselves.

Veterans often report negative perceptions of mental health care, reflected, for example, by a lack of trust in mental health professionals or concerns that treatment is ineffective or a last resort. Research shows that these negative perceptions are some of the strongest predictors of veterans' willingness to engage in mental health care. In essence, mental health care suffers from poor marketing and negative perceptions.

Part of the problem lies with the way in which mental health care is delivered. It can be off-putting to veterans who are in need of support but wary of sharing their experiences with anyone other than their battle buddies. Veterans sometimes feel that mental health professionals make judgments, such as whether a certain traumatic event warrants consideration in determining the diagnosis or which symptoms rise to the level of a "disorder".

Rather than talk about life experiences and responses using simple narrative processes, the mental health care approach tends to use a lot of medical or psychological labels. Normal reactions in a combat zone are considered "symptoms". Human emotions, such as grief, are measured by how "complex" they are. Ways of thinking that are ingrained in military training, such as high attention to detail, might be labeled "cognitive distortions". Helpful mental health advice is framed with phrases like, "You need to…", "Remember that…", "It is important for you to…", "Understand that…", "Realize that…", "Recognize that…", "Make sure you…". This is a language that implies that the professional knows what's best for the warrior, even though the warrior is the one who has to learn to live every day with the memories of what he or she experienced in the war zone.

When veterans make the difficult decision to overcome all obstacles and seek mental health care, they are looking for someone who is caring, competent, nonjudgmental, and available. Veterans prefer that communication is immediate, direct, and real. The mental health professional doesn't necessarily have to have military experience, although this certainly helps. It also helps to have some life experiences to draw from. Nevertheless, regardless of how much experience the health professionals have, they must be careful not to make assumptions or implicit judgements about a warrior's experience. Veterans often are looking for any excuse to leave treatment, and based on the data, veterans are walking every day.

In order to make a dent in this problem and bridge the gap in perspectives concerning war-related PTSD, I believe that both mental health professionals and veterans (and probably society at large) can benefit from greater understanding of the occupational context and paradox of war related PTSD, as well as understanding what post-deployment transition really means, and the relationship between PTSD and the biological and physiological processes expected in combat.

It is helpful to have a firm understanding of why the body continues to react as it did in the combat environment, even years later, and not automatically label these reactions pathological or psychological. It is important to understand PTSD both from a traditional medical model ("symptoms", "diagnosis", "treatment") as well as from the perspective of warriors ("responses", "skills", "occupational experiences"). The paradox of PTSD tells us something important about what it means to be human.

Transition and Readjustment from Deployment

There are many unrealistic expectations about the transition and readjustment period after returning from deployment. For active-duty brigade and regimental combat teams, there is an expectation that the entire unit will be able to "reset" and be ready for another deployment within a year. However, this is not sufficient for many warriors to fully re-engage with family members, integrate their experiences from the previous combat tour, modulate the physiological reactivity that continues after deployment, or learn to live with very difficult memories, particularly tragic events involving team members who are as close (or even closer) than the warrior's own family. Society asks a lot of our service members as it is; many veterans feel as if they are asked to suck it up and drive on when they get home.

The reality is that there is no normal period of transition. Deployment changes everyone in one way or another, and veterans need varying amounts of time to readjust. Many veterans grow from their deployment experiences, such as gaining greater maturity, wisdom, leadership and career opportunities, and an appreciation of the value of life and connections with loved ones. Some warriors make the transition quickly and smoothly. Others experience more lasting challenges. Readjustment growth and challenges can occur at the same time. They are not mutually exclusive.

Some readjustment challenges have to do with the nature of experiences downrange. War related experiences are myriad, but the events that understandably tend to have greater impact are those in which there were serious casualties involving unit members, collateral casualties, leadership failures, or feelings of betrayal. Accidents in the war zone can sometimes be as devastating as indirect or direct fire. Harassment, assault, or rape by a fellow service member— the ultimate form of betrayal in an environment where one totally depends on team members for protection and support—is particularly devastating.

Survivor's guilt and should've-would've-could've thinking are very common in veterans. There is a tendency to replay combat events over and over, thinking of ways that an outcome could have been changed—the illusion of choice. It is no wonder that many veterans find it difficult or impossible to move forward with life after war-zone experiences, and it's understandable for veterans to lock up these memories and emotions and avoid talking about them, especially with people who have never deployed.

Many Vietnam veterans are only now beginning to make the transition home in terms of addressing war-related experiences, more than thirty-five years after the end of that conflict.

Sometimes combat-related memories stay buried for years while life events such as marriage, raising children, and career take priority, but then resurface during a later life transition, such as after retirement, a marital separation, death of a family member, a stressful financial situation, illness, or kids leaving the home.

Warriors don't just stop being warriors when they get home. Once a warrior—always a warrior.

Transition takes time, but it's never too late to make a successful transition home, "successful" being defined as the ability to live with difficult deployment-related memories and also have productive employment or hobbies, meaningful relationships, personal growth, and the ability to experience joy in life.

Combat Physiology

All of the skills and reactions that serve important functions in survival of the team and success of the mission involve physiological processes. The extreme physical stress of deployment, sleep deprivation, and intensity of life-threatening experiences that can occur during deployment are associated with changes in how the body functions, including increased autonomic nervous system activation (higher adrenaline, faster reflexes), changes in levels of hormones that control different body functions (cortisol and others), and changes in how memory is processed. More attention goes to survival-related memories in deeper areas of the brain and less attention to thinking processes such as university studies or the list of things that has to be picked up from the grocery store. PTSD is associated with these physiological changes remaining in combat ready mode upon return home, and PTSD should be considered a physical condition as much as (or more than) a psychological or emotional condition.

As a result, veterans with PTSD have higher rates of virtually all categories of physical health problems than veterans without PTSD. That includes hypertension, cardiovascular disease, chronic pain in muscles or joints, headaches, gastrointestinal problems, sleep problems, and concentration or memory problems. Those with PTSD also end up on more medications and have more doctor visits.

Sometimes post-deployment physical symptoms such as headaches and memory and concentration problems are mistakenly attributed to previous head injuries (also called concussions or mTBIs), when they actually are caused by the physiological effects of combat. This has implications for delivering the correct treatment. All too often veterans are referred to different medical specialists and receive many diagnoses and multiple medications that increase the risk of side effects and adverse medication interactions. Having a strong primary care provider who can sort this out is crucial.

The bottom line is that going to war changes how the body functions, and the expectation that this will reset quickly upon return home is unrealistic. There is no switch to restore biological physiological functions back to the way they were before deployment. A dial is a better metaphor. It's best to understand these body responses from the perspective of how they serve important functions in a combat environment, and then look for ways to dial these responses down after returning home.

There are many ways to do this. I created a series of exercises and skills for navigating the transition home and dialing down combat-related reactions. However, each individual needs to find what works best for him or her.

Recovery and Treatment

Understanding transition and combat-related PTSD within an occupational and physiological context can help to put things in perspective, make sense of war-related responses, and guide treatment strategies. Having loving connections with friends and family is probably the single most beneficial factor. I can't say enough about the value of showing gratitude and appreciation for the people in your life whom you love. Peer-to-peer support programs with other veterans who have gone through similar experiences can be very beneficial. Having patience and a good sense of humor also helps enormously.

Veterans who receive treatment ideally should be given a range of choices based on what they are most comfortable with, so as to facilitate their willingness to remain in care. There are a variety of treatment options, and one size certainly does not fit all. Psychotherapy (talk therapy) is effective and leads to measurable improvements, including the physiological processes involved in PTSD. Although there are many variations of psychotherapy, virtually all of them involve three core components. The simpler and more direct approaches appear to work just as well as more complicated interventions. It's my belief that the more mental health professionals understand this, the more veterans will feel comfortable staying with care.

Being able to advocate for yourself to get your questions answered and find a provider you can work well with is important. The three core therapy components are:

Narration, probably the most important component, involves talking about the events that happened, as well as the emotions and thoughts connected with these experiences. Veterans are often reluctant to talk about their experiences because of the responses they get from people who haven't deployed and because the experiences can be connected with strong emotions. However, there is no better way to integrate these experiences and learn to live with difficult deployment related memories in a way that also allows for personal growth and finding meaning and joy in life. The narrative process is also very important for addressing difficult topics such as guilt, grief, or the illusion of choice.

Retraining the Body to face stressful situations involves exercises in which the veteran progressively visits locations that trigger strong responses (for example, crowded shopping malls) in order to retrain himself or herself not to have automatic combat-ready reactions in locations where the actual threat level is low.

Relaxation Exercises focus on dialing down the level of adrenaline, hyper-alertness, and improving sleep and concentration. This might involve diaphragmatic breathing and mindfulness meditation.

There is also a role for medications, particularly the selective serotonin reuptake inhibitors such as sertraline and paroxetine. Although not better than psychotherapy, they can be useful in alleviating symptoms, can be used along with psychotherapy, and are generally safe. Other medications also are prescribed to veterans with PTSD, with many considerations related to properly balancing potential benefits with risks. Two classes of medications that are widely used have been shown in several studies to have more risks than benefits. These include benzodiazepines (alprazolam, clonazepam, lorazepam, and diazepam) and atypical antipsychotics (risperidone, olanzapine, quetiapine, ziprasidone, aripiprazole).

Sometimes PTSD treatment is not successful because of ongoing physical health problems, such as musculoskeletal pain, headaches, or sleep disturbance, and it's necessary to address these problems first (or simultaneously). Sleep is not given nearly enough attention. The body tends to maintain combat-related sleep patterns after coming home (for example, sleeping much lighter, waking in the middle of the night, not feeling rested in the morning). It can sometimes take months or years for natural sleep processes to reestablish themselves.

There are many things that veterans can do to improve sleep, including modulating the intake of caffeine and alcohol. Veterans often continue to consume large quantities of caffeine after coming home without realizing how this can have a negative impact on sleep. They also sometimes reach for alcohol to help with sleep, without realizing that this can interfere with a successful transition. Although alcohol can seem to help at first, it actually makes sleep much worse by altering the normal stages of sleep necessary for restoration and health. REM sleep, the stage that involves dreaming, is initially suppressed by alcohol but then plays catch up as the alcohol wears off throughout the night, leading to a higher likelihood of waking up (and also having nightmares) in the middle of the night and not feeling rested in the morning.

The bottom line is that sometimes sleep won't return to normal until there is a lengthy alcohol-free period. Many medications that are prescribed for sleep (benzodiazepines, for example) are similar to alcohol and can actually make sleep or other PTSD symptoms worse over the long term.

A warrior doesn't stop being a warrior when he or she returns home from combat. Once a warrior, always a warrior. This has to do with rigorous military training, deployment-related experiences, what it means to be a warrior, and the physiological effects of war. If you would like to know more about navigating the transition home from deployment, things you can do to improve sleep, dial down combat-related reactions, or navigate the complex medical and mental health care system, I invite you to look further in my book, *Once a Warrior—Always a Warrior: Navigating the Transition from Combat to Home*. It's an honor to share my views with you, and I welcome your feedback at hoge@onceawarrior.com.

Retired Army Col. Charles W. Hoge, a medical doctor, directed the U.S. military's top research program on the mental health and neurological effects of the wars in

Afghanistan and Iraq from 2002-2009 at Walter Reed Army Institute of Research. He is the author of Once A Warrior—Always A Warrior: Navigating the Transition from Combat to Home (2010). *He deployed to Iraq in 2004. This article originally appearing in the* VVA Veteran, *Sept. / Oct. 2011, Reprinted with permission.*

IV. RECOVERY

Trauma and PTSD

by the Editors

As the men who've written here have told, there are many choices about how to spend one's time in prison. One of the consistent messages has been to educate one's self, to learn about what factors led a person to the behavior that got them imprisoned, and what they can do to change those factors in a positive direction. There are literally hundreds if not thousands of self-help programs and prison-sponsored programs available—many choices in some prisons, few choices in others. There is the prison mental health system, where counseling is available if one meets certain criteria. There is cognitive behavioral therapy (questioning one's beliefs and changing one's thinking) and exposure therapy (revisiting repressed traumatic events), two of the conventionally accepted forms of therapy. Treatment for substance abuse issues is also widely available. There are also many other types of classes and therapies with differing goals and strategies.

Simply reaching the point where one is willing to look at one's issues is generally regarded as a necessary first step, because denial really IS a powerful force. After that, there is tremendous variety of choices as to how to explore possibilities for healing and growth. These include everything from faith-based therapies, mindfulness meditation, nature-based therapies, Eastern body-based therapies such as the Prison Yoga Project, Western body-based therapies teaching somatic awareness; peer counseling in group therapy; stress and anger management skill training; victim awareness classes; creating a narrative of traumatic events through writings or art—the list is nearly endless. There are therapies that teach it's all about how you think; therapies that teach you it's all about how you pray; therapies that teach you to increase your body awareness; therapies that teach you must mourn and grieve your losses to deal with the effects of trauma, therapies that try to take into account all these things. And of course, there is the therapeutic strategy that motivated Doc and Ed and is the motto of the VSO and the motivation for this book: 'helping ourselves by helping others.

No single approach seems to be a good fit for everybody. You have to feel your own way for where you feel safe enough to begin the journey of dealing with issues that have previously stayed hidden, outside of your awareness.

The men who have written for this book have an average incarcerated time of more than 20 years. They have been exposed to many teachings from various prison-sponsored and self-help programs. In this section, we have included writings by outside professionals. The men nominated these writings to be included here because they found them to contain extremely useful information. Ideas and practices which helped them gain insight and positive movement forward in their individual trauma recovery journeys. A type of 'Consumer Reports' collection of good things to know as one approaches the task of healing. It is by no means an all-inclusive list, it is a guidepost from men who have worked hard to correct their character defects and have changed from their troubled pasts. From all of us who have worked to put this together, we hope you give these teachings your attention and they help inspire you to move forward in your journey as they have helped those who came before you. We are witnesses that this kind of profound change really is possible.

One of the most useful tools for many participants has been to become trauma-informed; that is, to learn how overwhelming experiences and difficult life situations can greatly influence one's attitudes, beliefs, and behavior, and lead to the development of Post-Traumatic Stress Disorder (PTSD) and—in the case of ongoing and repeated traumas—Complex PTSD (C-PTSD). In this section we offer information to help you learn about what PTSD really is, its impact and symptoms, and some things one can do to ease living with this condition. The PTSD Checklist self-rating instrument developed by the Department of Veterans Affairs is one way to get started. With it, you can check the intensity of your own symptoms (if any) and this assists in evaluating for yourself if in fact PTSD may be operating in your life. Only a clinician can make an official diagnosis of PTSD.

The PTSD Checklist (PCL-5)

How is the PCL-5 scored and interpreted? Respondents are asked to rate how bothered they have been by each of 20 items in the past month on a 5- point Likert scale ranging from 0-4.

Items are summed to provide a total severity score (range = 0-80). 0 = Not at all 1 = A little bit 2 = Moderately 3 = Quite a bit 4 = Extremely The PCL-5 can determine a provisional diagnosis in two ways: • Summing all 20 items (range 0-80) and using a cut-point score of 31-33 appears to be reasonable based upon current psychometric work. However, when choosing a cutoff score, it is essential to consider the goals of the assessment and the population being assessed. The lower the cutoff score, the more lenient the criteria for inclusion, increasing the possible number of false-positives. The higher the cutoff score, the more stringent the inclusion criteria and the more potential for false-negatives. • Treating each item rated as 2 = "Moderately" or higher as a symptom endorsed, then following the DSM-5 diagnostic rule which requires at least: 1 Criterion B item (questions 1-5), 1 Criterion C item (questions 6-7), 2 Criterion D items (questions 8-14), 2 Criterion E items (questions 15-20). In general, use of a cutoff score tends to produce more reliable results than the DSM-5 diagnostic rule. If a patient meets a provisional diagnosis using either of the methods above, he or she needs further assessment (e.g., CAPS-5) to confirm a diagnosis of PTSD.

Instructions: Below is a list of problems that people sometimes have in response to a very stressful experience. Please read each problem on the following pages carefully and then circle one of the numbers to the right to indicate how much you have been bothered by that problem in the past month.

In the past month, how much were you bothered by:	Not at all	A little bit	Moderate	Quite a bit	Extremely
1. Repeated, disturbing, and unwanted memories of the stressful experience?	0	1	2	3	4
2. Repeated, disturbing dreams of the stressful experience?	0	1	2	3	4
3. Suddenly feeling or acting as if the stressful experience were actually happening again (as if you were actually back there reliving it)?	0	1	2	3	4
4. Feeling very upset when something reminded you of the stressful experience?	0	1	2	3	4
5. Having strong physical reactions when something reminded you of the stressful experience (for example, heart pounding, trouble breathing, sweating)?	0	1	2	3	4
6. Avoiding memories, thoughts, or feelings related to the stressful experience?	0	1	2	3	4
7. Avoiding external reminders of the stressful experience (for example, people, places, conversations, activities, objects, or situations)?	0	1	2	3	4

8. Trouble remembering important parts of the stressful experience?	0	1	2	3	4
9. Having strong negative beliefs about yourself, other people, or the world (for example, having thoughts such as: I am bad, there is something seriously wrong with me, no one can be trusted, the world is completely dangerous)?	0	1	2	3	4
10. Blaming yourself or someone else for the stressful experience or what happened after it?	0	1	2	3	4
11. Having strong negative feelings such as fear, horror, anger, guilt, or shame?	0	1	2	3	4
12. Loss of interest in activities that you used to enjoy?	0	1	2	3	4
13. Feeling distant or cut off from other people?	0	1	2	3	4
14. Trouble experiencing positive feelings (for example, being unable to feel happiness or have loving feelings for people close to you)?	0	1	2	3	4
15. Irritable behavior, angry outbursts, or acting aggressively?	0	1	2	3	4
16. Taking too many risks or doing things that could cause you harm?	0	1	2	3	4

17. Being "superalert" or watchful or on guard?	0	1	2	3	4
18. Feeling jumpy or easily startled?	0	1	2	3	4
19. Having difficulty concentrating?	0	1	2	3	4
20. Trouble falling or staying asleep?	0	1	2	3	4

The NATIONAL CENTER FOR PTSD has made available the PTSD CHECKLIST for DSM-5, Version date: 14 August, 2013 Reference: Weathers, F.W., Litz, B.T., Keane, T. M., Palmijeri, P.A., Marx, B.P., & Schnurr, P.P. (2013). The PTSD Checklist for DSM-5 (PCL-5) Standard {Measurement instrument}. Available from http://www.ptsd.va..gov/

Twelve Life Impacting Symptoms— Complex PTSD Survivors Can Endure

by Lilly Hope Lucario

Complex trauma is still a relatively new field of psychology. Complex post-traumatic stress disorder (C-PTSD) results from enduring complex trauma.

Complex trauma is ongoing or repeated interpersonal trauma, where the victim is traumatized in captivity, and where there is no perceived way to escape. Ongoing child abuse is captivity abuse because the child cannot escape. Domestic violence is another example. Forced prostitution/sex trafficking is another.

Complex PTSD is a proposed disorder which is different from post-traumatic stress disorder.

Many of the issues and symptoms endured by complex trauma survivors are outside of the list of symptoms within the (uncomplicated) PTSD diagnostic criteria. Complex PTSD does acknowledge and validate these added symptoms.

The impact of complex trauma is very different to a one-time or short-lived trauma. The effect of ongoing/repeated trauma—caused by people—changes the brain, and also changes the survivor at a core level. It changes the way survivors view the world, other people, and themselves in profound ways.

The following are some of the symptoms and impacts most felt by complex trauma survivors:

1. Deep Fear of Trust

People who endure ongoing abuse, particularly from significant people in their lives, develop an intense and understandable fear of trusting people. If the abuse was parents or caregivers, this intensifies. Ongoing trauma wires the brain for fear and distrust. It becomes the way the brain copes with any further potential abuse. Complex trauma survivors often find trusting people to be very difficult, and it takes little for any trust built to be destroyed. The brain senses issues and this overwhelms the already severely-traumatized brain. This fear of trust is extremely impactful on a survivor's life. Trust can be learned with support and an understanding of trusting people slowly and carefully.

2. Terminal Aloneness

This is a phrase I used to describe to my counselor the terribly painful aloneness I have always felt as a complex trauma survivor. Survivors often feel so little connection and trust with people, they remain in a terrible state of aloneness, even when surrounded by people. I described it once as having a glass wall between myself and other people. I can see them, but I cannot connect with them.

Another issue that increases this aloneness is feeling different than other people. Feeling damaged, broken and unable to be like other people can haunt a survivor, increasing the loneliness.

3. Emotion Regulation

Intense emotions are common with complex trauma survivors. It is understandable that ongoing abuse can cause many different and intense emotions. This is normal for complex trauma survivors.

Learning to manage and regulate emotions is vital in being able to manage all the other symptoms.

4. Emotional Flashbacks

Flashbacks are something all PTSD survivors may can deal with and there are three types:

Visual flashbacks—-where your mind is triggered and transported back to the trauma, and you feel as if you are reliving it.

Somatic Flashbacks—where the survivor feels sensations, pain and discomfort in areas of the body affected by the trauma. This pain/sensation cannot be explained by any other health issues and are triggered by something that creates the body to 'feel' the trauma again.

Emotional Flashbacks—The least known and understood, yet the type complex trauma survivors an experience the most. These are where emotions from the past are triggered. Often the survivor does not understand these intense emotions are flashbacks, and it appears the survivor is being irrationally emotional. When I learned about emotional flashbacks, it was a huge light bulb moment of finally understanding why I have intense emotions, when they do not reflect the issue occurring now, but in fact emotions felt during the trauma, being triggered. But there is no visual of the trauma—as with visual flashbacks. So, it takes a lot of work to start to understand, when experiencing emotional flashbacks.

For more information about emotional flashbacks, see my articles on my website.

5. Hypervigilance: About People

Most people with PTSD have hypervigilance, where the person scans the environment for potential risks and likes to have their back to the wall.

But complex trauma survivors often have a deep subconscious need to 'work people out'. Since childhood I have been aware of people's non-verbal cues; body language, tone of voice, and their facial expressions. I also subconsciously learn people's habits and store away what they say. Then if anything occurs that contradicts any of this, it will immediately flag as something potentially dangerous.

This can be exhausting. And it can create a deep skill set of discernment about people. The aim of healing fear-based hypervigilance is turning into non-fear-based discernment.

6. Loss of Faith

Complex trauma survivors often endure a loss of faith. This can be about people, about the world being good, about religion, and a loss of faith about self.

Complex trauma survivors often view the world as dangerous and people as all potentially abusive, which is understandable when having endured ongoing severe abuse. Many complex trauma survivors walk away from their religious beliefs. For example, to believe in a good and loving God who allows suffering and heinous abuse to occur can feel like the ultimate betrayal. This is something needing considerable compassion.

7. Profoundly Hurt Inner Child

Childhood complex trauma survivors often have a very hurt inner child that continues on to affect the survivor in adulthood. When a child's emotional needs are not met, and a child is repeatedly hurt and abused, this deeply and profoundly affects the child's development. A survivor will often continue on subconsciously wanting the unmet childhood needs in adulthood. Looking for safety, protection, being cherished and loved, can often be normal unmet needs in childhood, and the survivor searches for these in other adults. This can be where survivors search for mother and father figures. Transference issues in counseling can occur and this is normal for childhood abuse survivors.

Inner child healing can be healing for childhood abuse survivors. It is where the survivor begins to meet the needs of their hurt and wounded child, themselves. I have further info about this on my website.

8. Helplessness and Toxic Shadow

Due to enduring ongoing or repeated abuse, the survivor can develop a sense of hopelessness—that nothing will ever be OK. They can feel so profoundly damaged, they see no hope for anything to get better. When faced with long periods of abuse or trauma that stops, the survivor can continue on having these deep core-level beliefs of hopelessness. This intensifies by the terribly

175

life-impacting symptoms of complex PTSD that keep the survivor stuck with the trauma, with little hope of this easing. Toxic shame is a common issue survivors of complex trauma endure. Often the perpetrators of the abuse make the survivor feel they don't deserve to be treated any better.

Sexual abuse can create a whole added layer of toxic shame, which requires very specific and compassionate therapy, if this is accessible. Often, sexual abuse survivors who are repeatedly enduring this heinous abuse can develop feelings of being dirty, damaged, and disgusting when their bodies are violated in this way.

9. Repeated Search For a Rescuer

Subconsciously looking for someone to rescue them is something many survivors understandably think about during the ongoing trauma and thus can continue on after the trauma has ceased. The survivor can feel helpless and yearn for someone to come and rescue them from the pain they feel and want them to make their lives better. This sadly often leads to the survivor seeking out the wrong types of people and being retraumatized repeatedly.

10. Dissociation

When enduring ongoing abuse, the brain can utilize dissociation as a coping method. This can be from daydreaming to more life-impacting forms of dissociation such as dissociative identity disorder (DID). This is particularly experienced by child abuse survivors, who are emotionally unable to cope with trauma in the same way an adult can.

For more information about the different types of dissociation, see my website.

11. Persistent Sadness and Being Suicidal

Complex trauma survivors often experience ongoing states of sadness and severe depression. Mood disorders are often co-morbid with complex PTSD.

Complex trauma survivors are high risk for suicidal thoughts, suicidal ideation, and being actively suicidal. Suicidal ideation can become a way of coping, where the survivor feels like they have a way to end the severe pain if it becomes any worse. Often, the deep emotional pain survivors feel, can feel unbearable. This is when survivors are at risk of developing suicidal thoughts.

For more information about suicidal issues, see my website.

12. Muscle Armoring

Many complex trauma survivors who have experienced ongoing abuse develop body hypervigilance. This is where the body is continually tensed, as though the body is 'braced' for potential trauma. This leads to pain issues as the muscles are being overworked. Chronic pain and other issues related such as chronic fatigue and fibromyalgia can result. Massage, guided muscle relaxation and other ways to manage this can help.

All of these issues are very normal for complex trauma survivors. Enduring complex trauma is not a normal life experience, and therefore the consequences it creates are different, yet very normal for what they have experienced and endured.

Not every survivor will endure all these, and there are other symptoms that can be endured. I always suggest trauma-informed counseling, if that is accessible. There are medications available to help with symptoms such as anxiety and depression.

There are also many self-help strategies to manage the symptoms and help heal. Many of these are listed on my website. Lastly, I advise that empathy, gentleness, and compassion are required for complex trauma survivors.

Lilly Hope Lucario, self-described as a 'severe and multiple complex trauma survivor', operates a website at https://healingfromcomplextraumaandptsd.wordpress.com/category/lilly-hope-lucario/ with trauma-informed content. Reprinted with permission.

Meditation on Being a Baby Killer

by Michael Parmeley

We knew that we killed them
Although no one had said it,
The terrified mother
Clutching terrified child.
Big Sherman, my gunner, Said he couldn't continue.
He'd looked in the bunker.
He started to cry.
I tell him, "It happens.
No one had meant it.
It happens in war.
We have to move on."

Time passes, much later;
The bunker's behind me.
In my mind I revisit. I try to move on.
Somewhere inside me
Big Sherman is crying.
I tell him it happens.
I tell myself too.

There's a myth of recovery,
That you put it all behind you,
Remember the good times,
Let bad memories fade.
But memories aren't like that.

Like bones they help build you.
They stand up to be counted.
They're part of what's true.

And now I' a writer,
I put words down on paper;
Like baby and bunker And terrified mother.

I know that we killed them.
No one need say it.
I know that they're dying Right now as I speak.

A mother and child,
Alone in a bunker,
A war passing over,
Right now as I speak.

This emotionally intense poem was written by Vietnam veteran Michael Parmeley, who traveled to Vietnam many years after the war and made a prayer at a previous battle site with former enemy combatants in honor of the fallen from all sides. Originally appearing in Veterans of War, Veterans of Peace, *reprinted with permission of the author. Doc Piper's commentary on this: "I could have written that".*

Why We Should All Care About Psychological Trauma

by Michelle Stevens, Ph.D

I have a client named "Rozlyn" who is attempting to leave an abusive marriage. Her husband, "Bill," is combat veteran who served in Desert Storm. Before the war, Bill was apparently easygoing. When he came back, though, he was different—angry, detached, alcoholic. Rozlyn and Bill have two grown children who both witnessed alcoholism and violence throughout their childhoods. Their son, "Billy," often got into trouble at school. By seventh grade, he was committing petty crimes. Billy is now serving a life sentence for the murder of a sales clerk during a botched robbery. The couple's daughter, "Ashley," hasn't fared much better. After being sexually abused by her drunk father, she ran away from home at the age of fourteen. She became addicted to drugs and had three children out of wedlock, all of whom are now in foster care. There's no doubt that Rozlyn's story is tragic. Her family has been marred by violence, alcoholism, drug addiction, and unplanned pregnancies, and chances are strong that her grandchildren will continue this downward spiral of hopeless dysfunction. Along the way, their problematic behaviors will tax our overburdened legal, healthcare, education, and social service systems, leading our country into ever-increasing debt and crisis.

How to handle people like Bill, Rozlyn and their offspring has been publicly debated for years.

Out of that debate has come solutions such as Prohibition...and repeal, the war on drugs...and legalized pot, Planned Parenthood...and abstinence education, three strikes...and overflowing prisons. But despite all our attempts to solve society's ills, they don't go away. The generational cycle of despair goes on and on. Perhaps that's because we're approaching these problems all wrong. Instead of viewing addiction, domestic violence, sexual abuse, unplanned pregnancies, and crime as separate issues, we need to look at the root cause.

More often than not, that root cause is psychological trauma. Psychological trauma is what happens to people after they have experienced violence—from things like war, domestic abuse, child abuse, and crime. It negatively affects people in profound and permanent ways. Consider these findings: Up to 30% of veterans who suffer trauma in war eventually develop prolonged cases of PTSD. [i] Research indicates that 39% of veterans are alcoholics and 3% abuse drugs. [ii] Combat veterans are responsible for 21% of all domestic abuse cases nationwide.

Childhood trauma—such as having an alcoholic parent and/or witnessing domestic violence— causes a range of psychological, emotional, and physical problems. One long-term study found that up to 80% of abused people had a least one psychiatric disorder at age 21.[iii] PTSD, borderline personality disorder, dissociative disorders, depression, and anxiety are all linked to a history of child abuse, as are eating disorders, sexual problems (including teen pregnancy), addiction, ADHD, learning disabilities, self-harm behaviors, and a propensity for victimization in adulthood. Boys who were abused in childhood are twice as likely to commit crimes. It is estimated that crime indirectly induced by abuse costs society between $6.7-$62.5 billion a year. [iv]

Considering all the collateral damage that is done by trauma, it's not an overstatement to say that psychological trauma may be the single biggest factor negatively affecting our society. Yet, I've never heard the term "psychological trauma" used in the mainstream media, and it's rarely considered as a factor in the educational or legal systems. While social service and mental health professionals sometimes factor in trauma, it is rarely given the weight it deserves.

This is a shame, because when people are properly informed about the effects of trauma—and use that knowledge to deal with problematic, traumatized people—positive changes occur. In Washington state, for instance, a trauma-informed approach with misbehaving students has led to an 85% reduction in suspension rates. [v] Using a trauma-informed approach with incarcerated juvenile delinquents has been shown to lower recidivism. [vi]

Imagine if Bill had been properly treated for the effects of trauma after he'd come home from war. It may have curbed his alcoholism and abusive behavior toward his wife and kids. If the kids had not grown up in an abusive home, chances are they wouldn't have moved into lives of addiction and crime. The penal system would have one less inmate. The legal would have one less murder victim and one less murder victim's family. The foster care system would have three less kids bringing problems into the educational and mental health systems. The cycle goes on and on. If we, as a society, could wake up to the fact that psychological trauma is the root cause of many of our problems, we could institute trauma-informed approaches in our legal, health, social service, and educational systems. Then, perhaps, our interventions might actually do some good. I hope we do. Otherwise, the cost—in money and lives—is just too high.

[i] Ramchand, R., Schell, T., Karney, B., Osilla, K., Burns, R. & Caldarone, L. (2010). Disparate prevalence estimates of PTSD among service members who served in Iraq and Afghanistan: possible explanations. Journal of Traumatic Stress, 23(1), 59–68.

[ii] Eisen, S., Schultz, M., Vogt, D., Glickman, M., Elwy, A., Drainoni, M., et al. (2012). Mental and physical health status and alcohol and drug use following return from deployment to Iraq or Afghanistan. American Journal of Public Health, 102, 66–73.

[iii] Silverman, A., Reinherz, H. & Giaconia, R. (1996). The long-term sequelae of child and adolescent abuse: a longitudinal community study. Child Abuse and Neglect, 20(8), 709-23.

[iv] Currie, J. & Tekin, E. (2006) Does child abuse cause crime? [working paper No. 12171] The National Bureau of Economic Research.

[v] Stevens, J. (2012, April 13). Lincoln High School in Walla Walla, WA, tries new approach to school discipline—suspensions drop 85%. ACEs Too High.

[vi] Griffin, G, Germain, E. & Wilkerson, R. (2012). Using a trauma-informed approach in juvenile justice institutions. Journal of Child & Adolescent Trauma, 5(3), 271-283.

Originally published in Psychology Today, 2/28/17. Reprinted with permission.

Healing The Shame Of Child Abuse Through Self- Compassion

by Beverly Engel, L.M.F.T.

"Shame is the lie someone told you about yourself."
Anais Nin (attributed)

Several months ago I wrote a blog on how self-compassion can heal the shame of childhood wounds and I received many queries about shame and self-compassion from *Psychology Today* readers. I'm happy to announce that my book, *It Wasn't Your Fault: Freeing Yourself of the Shame of Childhood Abuse with the Power of Self-Compassion*, has just been published (New Harbinger). I'd like to address some of your queries and share some of the major ideas in the book with you here.

If you were a victim of childhood abuse or neglect, you know about shame. You have likely been plagued by it all your life without identifying it as shame. You may feel shame because you blame yourself for the abuse itself ("My father wouldn't have hit me if I had minded him"), or because you felt such humiliation at having been abused ("I feel like such a wimp for not defending myself"). While those who were sexually abused tend to suffer from the most shame, those who suffered from physical, verbal, or emotional abuse blame themselves as well. In the case of child sexual abuse, no matter how many times you have heard the words "It's not your fault," the chances are high that you still blame yourself in some way—for being submissive, for not telling someone and having the abuse continue, for "enticing" the abuser with your behavior or dress, or because you felt some physical pleasure.

In the case of physical, verbal, and emotional abuse, you may blame yourself for "not listening" and thus making your parent or other caretakers angry that he or she yelled at you or hit you. Children tend to blame the neglect and abuse they experience on themselves, in essence saying to themselves, "My mother is treating me like this because I've been bad," or, "I am being neglected because I am unlovable." As an adult you may have continued this kind of rationalization, putting up with poor treatment by others because you believe you brought it on yourself. Conversely, when good things happen to you, you may actually become uncomfortable, because you feel so unworthy.

Former victims of child abuse are typically changed by the experience, not only because they were traumatized, but because they feel a loss of innocence and dignity and they carry forward a heavy burden of shame. Emotional, physical, and sexual child abuse can so overwhelm a victim with shame that it actually comes to define the person, keeping her from her full potential. It can cause a victim both to remain fixed at the age he was at the time of his victimization and to repeat the abuse over and over in his lifetime.

You may also have a great deal of shame due to the exposure of the abuse. If you reported the abuse to someone, you may blame yourself for the consequences of your outcry— your parents divorcing, your molester going to jail, your family going to court.

And there is the shame you may feel about your behavior that was a consequence of the abuse. Former victims of childhood abuse tend to feel a great deal of shame for things they did as children as a result of the abuse. For example, perhaps unable to express their anger at an abuser, they may have taken their hurt and anger out on those who were smaller or weaker than themselves, such as younger siblings. They may have become bullies at school, been belligerent toward authority figures, or started stealing, taking drugs, or otherwise acting out against society. In the case of sexual abuse, former victims may have continued the cycle of abuse by introducing younger children to sex.

You may also feel shame because of things you have done as an adult to hurt yourself and others, such as abusing alcohol or drugs, becoming sexually promiscuous, or breaking the law, not realizing that these types of behavior were a result of the abuse you suffered.

Unbeknownst to them, adults who were abused as children often express the overwhelming shame they feel by pushing away those who try to be good to them; by sabotaging their success; by becoming emotionally or physically abusive to their partners; or by continuing a pattern of being abused or subjecting their own children to witnessing abuse. Former abuse victims may repeat the cycle of abuse by emotionally, physically, or sexually abusing their own children, or may abandon their children because they can't take care of them.

Shame can affect literally every aspect of a former victim's life, from your self-confidence, self-esteem, and body image to your ability to relate to others, navigate intimate relationships, and be a good parent to your work performance, ability to be learn new things, and ability to care for yourself. Shame is responsible for myriad personal problems, including: self-criticism and self-blame; self-neglect; self-destructive behaviors (such as abusing your body with food, alcohol, drugs, or cigarettes, self-mutilation, or being accident-prone); perfectionism (based on fear of being caught in a mistake); believing you don't deserve good things; believing if others really knew you they would dislike or be disgusted by you (commonly known as the "imposter syndrome"); people-pleasing and co-dependent behavior; tending to be critical of others (trying to give shame away); intense rage (frequent physical fights or road rage); and acting out against society (breaking rules or laws).

Shame from childhood abuse almost always manifests itself in one or more of these ways:

- It causes former abuse victims to abuse themselves with critical self-talk, alcohol or drug abuse, destructive eating patterns, and/or other forms of self-harm. Two-thirds of people in treatment for drug abuse reported being abused or neglected as children (Swon 1998).
- It causes former abuse victims to develop victim-like behavior, whereby they expect and accept unacceptable, abusive behavior from others. As many as 90 percent of women in battered women's shelters report having been abused or neglected as children (U.S. Department of Health and Human Services 2013).

- It causes abuse victims to become abusive. About 30 percent of abused and neglected children will later abuse their own children (U.S. Department of Health and Human Services 2013).

The truth is that for most former victims of childhood abuse, shame is likely one of the worst effects of the abuse. Unless you heal this pervasive shame, you will likely continue to suffer from its effects throughout your lifetime.

Facing the problems that shame has created in your life can be daunting. You may be overwhelmed with the problem of how to heal the shame caused by the childhood abuse you experienced. The good news is that there is a way to heal your shame so that you can begin to see the world through different eyes—eyes not clouded by the perception that you are "less than," inadequate, damaged, worthless, or unlovable.

The Healing Power of Self-Compassion

Like a poison, toxic shame needs to be neutralized by another substance—an antidote—if the patient is to be saved. Compassion is the only thing that can counteract the isolating, stigmatizing, debilitating poison of shame.

Many of you may be aware of the writings of Alice Miller. Miller believes that what victims of childhood abuse need most is what she called a "compassionate witness" to validate their experiences and support them through their pain (Miller 1984). For many years I have personally experienced how healing my being a compassionate witness is for my clients, as well as how transformative my having a compassionate therapist had been for me.

In recent years, many others, including major researchers have taken up the subject of compassion. Their work has revealed, among other insights, that the kindness, support, encouragement, and compassion of others have a huge impact on how our brains, bodies, and general sense of well-being develop. Love and kindness, especially in early life, even affect how some of our genes are expressed (Gilbert 2009, Cozolino 2007).

The Research on Self-Compassion

By studying much of the research on compassion, I discovered that while I had come to understand the healing powers of compassion, I hadn't truly recognized the importance of self compassion—extending compassion to oneself in instances of perceived inadequacy, failure, or general suffering—in the treatment of psychotherapy clients, particularly former victims of child abuse. In 2003, Kristin Neff published the first two articles defining and measuring self compassion (Neff 2003a, Neff 2003b); before this, the subject of self-compassion had never been formally studied. There have since been over two hundred journal articles and dissertations on self-compassion.

One of the most consistent findings in this research literature is that greater self-compassion is linked to less psychopathology (Barnard and Curry 2011). And a recent meta-analysis showed self-compassion to have a positive effect on depression, anxiety, and stress across twenty studies (MacBeth and Gumley 2012).

Self-compassion also appears to facilitate resilience by moderating people's reactions to negative events—trauma in particular. Gilbert and Procter (2001) suggest that self-compassion provides emotional resilience because it deactivates the threat system. And it has been found that abused individuals with higher levels of self-compassion are better able to cope with upsetting events (Vettese et al. 2011).

There is also evidence that self-compassion helps people diagnosed with post-traumatic stress disorder (PTSD). In one study of college students who showed PTSD symptoms after experiencing a traumatic event such as an accident or life-threatening illness, those with more self-compassion showed less severe symptoms than those who lacked self-compassion. In particular, they were less likely to display signs of emotional avoidance and more comfortable facing the thoughts, feelings, and sensations associated with the trauma they experienced (Thompson and Waltz 2008).

Finally, in addition to self-compassion being a key factor in helping those who were traumatized in childhood, it turns out that self-compassion is the missing key to alleviating shame.

Confirming what I knew from my extensive work with former victims of child abuse, research shows that traumatized individuals feel significant levels of shame and/or guilt (Jonsson and Segesten 2004). Shame has been recognized as a major component of a range of mental health problems and proneness to aggression (Gilbert 1997, Gilbert 2003, Gilligan 2003, Tangney and Dearing 2002). And it has been found that decreases in anxiety, shame, and guilt and increases in the willingness to express sadness, anger, and closeness were associated with higher levels of self-compassion (Germer and Neff 2013).

One clinician, Paul Gilbert, author of "The Compassionate Mind," found that self-compassion helped to alleviate both shame and self-judgment. A study of the effectiveness of Gilbert's Compassionate Mind Training (CMT), a group-based therapy model that works specifically with shame, guilt, and self-blame, found that the training resulted in significant reductions in depression, self-attacking, feelings of inferiority, and shame (Gilbert and Procter 2006).

In addition, research suggests that self-compassion can act as an antidote to self-criticism—a major characteristic of those who experience intense shame (Gilbert and Miles 2000). Self compassion is a powerful trigger for the release of oxytocin, the hormone that increases feelings of trust, calm, safety, generosity, and connectedness. Self-criticism has a very different effect on our bodies. The amygdala, the oldest part of the brain, is designed to quickly detect threats in the environment. These trigger the fight-or-flight response—the amygdala sends signals that increase blood pressure, adrenaline, and cortisol, mobilizing the strength and energy needed to confront or avoid the threat. Although this system was designed by evolution to deal with physical attacks, it is activated just as readily by emotional attacks—from ourselves and others. Over time, increased cortisol levels deplete neurotransmitters involved in the ability to experience pleasure, leading to depression (Gilbert 2005).

Neurological evidence also shows that self-kindness (a major component of self-compassion) and self-criticism operate quite differently in terms of brain function. A recent study examined reactions to personal failure using fMRI (functional magnetic resonance imaging) technology.

While in a brain scanner, participants were presented with hypothetical situations such as "A third job rejection letter in a row arrives in the post." They were then told to imagine reacting to the situation in either a kind or a self-critical way. Self-criticism was associated with activity in the lateral prefrontal cortex and dorsal anterior cingulate—areas of the brain associated with error processing and problem solving. Being kind and reassuring toward oneself was associated with left temporal pole and insula activation—areas of the brain associated with positive emotions and compassion (Longe et al. 2009). As Kristin Neff (2011) aptly stated, "Instead of seeing ourselves as a problem to be fixed…self-kindness allows us to see ourselves as valuable human beings who are worthy of care."

Of particular interest to me was recent research in the neurobiology of compassion as it relates to shame—namely that we now know some of the neurobiological correlates of feeling unlovable and how shame gets stuck in our neural circuitry. Moreover, and most crucially of all, due to our brains' capacity to grow new neurons and new synaptic connections, we can proactively repair (and re-pair) old shame memories with new experiences of self-empathy and self-compassion.

In light of my research, I determined that in addition to offering my clients compassion for their suffering, I needed to teach them how to practice self-compassion on an ongoing basis in order to heal the many layers of shame they experienced.

Combining what I learned about compassion and self-compassion with the wisdom I've gleaned from my many years of working with victims of childhood abuse, I created a program specifically aimed at helping those who experienced abuse become free of debilitating shame. My Compassion Cure program combines groundbreaking scientific research on self-compassion, compassion, shame, and restorative justice with real-life case examples (modified to protect the subjects' anonymity). Its proprietary processes and exercises help abuse victims reduce or eliminate the shame that has weighed them down and kept them stuck in the past.

By learning to practice self-compassion, you will rid yourself of shame-based beliefs, such as you are worthless, defective, bad, or unlovable. Abuse victims often cope with these false yet powerful beliefs by trying to ignore them or convince themselves otherwise by puffing themselves up, overachieving, or becoming perfectionistic. These strategies take huge amounts of energy, and they are not effective. Rather, actively approaching, recognizing, validating, and understanding shame is the way to overcome it.

Debilitating Shame

"Shame is sickness of the soul."
Silvan Tomkins

While many people suffer from shame, not everyone suffers from what is referred to as debilitating shame. Debilitating shame is shame that is so all consuming that it negatively affects every aspect of a person's life—his perceptions of himself, his relationship with others, her ability to be intimate with a romantic partner, her ability to raise children in a healthy manner, his ability to risk and achieve success in his career, and her overall physical and emotional health. The following questionnaire will help you determine whether you suffer from debilitating shame.

Questionnaire: Do You Suffer from Debilitating Shame Due to Childhood Abuse?

1. Do you blame yourself for the abuse you experienced as a child?
2. Do you believe your parent (or other adult or older child) wouldn't have abused you if you hadn't pushed him or her into doing it?
3. Do you believe you were a difficult, stubborn, or selfish child who deserved the abuse you received?
4. Do you believe you made it difficult for your parents or others to love you?
5. Do you believe you were a disappointment to your parents or family?
6. Do you feel you are basically unlovable?

7. Do you have a powerful inner critic who finds fault with nearly everything you do?

8. Are you a perfectionist?

9. Do you believe you don't deserve to be happy, loved, or successful?

10. Do you have a difficult time believing someone could love you?

11. Do you push away people who are good to you?

12. Are you afraid that if people really get to know you they won't like or accept you? Do you feel like a fraud?

13. Do you believe that anyone who likes or loves you has something wrong with them?

14. Do you feel like a failure in life?

15. Do you hate yourself?

16. Do you feel ugly—inside and out?

17. Do you hate your body?

18. Do you believe that the only way someone can like you is if you do everything they want?

19. Are you a people pleaser?

20. Do you censor yourself when you talk to other people, always being careful not to offend them or hurt their feelings?

21. Do you feel like the only thing you have to offer is your sexuality?

22. Are you addicted to alcohol, drugs, sex, pornography, shopping, gambling, or stealing, or do you suffer from any other addiction?

23. Do you find it nearly impossible to admit when you are wrong or when you've made a mistake?

24. Do you feel bad about the way you've treated people?

25. Are you afraid of what you're capable of doing?

26. Are you afraid of your tendency to be abusive—either verbally, emotionally, physically, or sexually?

27. Have you been in one or more relationships where you were abused either verbally, emotionally, physically, or sexually?

28. Did you or do you feel you deserved the abuse?

29. Do you always blame yourself if something goes wrong in a relationship?

30. Do you feel like it isn't worth trying because you'll only fail?
31. Do you sabotage your happiness, your relationships, or your success?
32. Are you self-destructive (engaging in acts of self-harm, driving recklessly, suicidal attempts, and so on)?
33. Do you feel inferior to or less than other people?
34. Do you often lie about your accomplishments or your history in order to make yourself look better in others' eyes?
35. Do you neglect your body, your health, or your emotional needs (not eating right, not getting enough sleep, not taking care of your medical or dental needs)?

There isn't any formal scoring for this questionnaire, but if you answered yes to many of these questions, you can be assured that you are suffering from debilitating shame. If you answered yes to just a few, it is still evident that you have an issue with shame.

Shame is Not a Singular Experience

Just as the source of shame can be all forms of abuse or neglect, shame is not just one feeling but many. It is a cluster of feelings and experiences. These can include:

Feelings of being humiliated. Abuse is always humiliating to the victim, but some types are more humiliating than others. Certainly, sexual abuse almost always has an element of humiliation to it, since it is a violation of very private body parts and since there is a knowing on the child's part that incest and/or sex between a child and an adult is taboo. (These taboos hold in nearly every culture in the world.) If the abuse involves public exposure—for example, being chastised or physically punished in front of others, particularly peers—the element of humiliation can be quite profound.

Feelings of impotence. When a child realizes there is nothing he can do to stop the abuse, he feels powerless, helpless. This can also lead to his always feeling unsafe, even long after the abuse has stopped.

Feelings of being exposed. Abuse and the accompanying feelings of vulnerability and helplessness cause the child to feel self-conscious and exposed—seen in a painfully diminished way. The fact that he could not stop the abuse makes him feel weak and exposed both to himself and to anyone present.

Feelings of being defective or less-than. Most victims of abuse report feeling defective, damaged, or corrupted following the experience of being abused.

Feelings of alienation and isolation. What follows the trauma of abuse is the feeling of suddenly being different, less-than, damaged, or cast out. And while victims may long to talk to someone about their inner pain, they often feel immobilized, trapped, and alone in their shame.

Feelings of self-blame. Victims almost always blame themselves for being abused and being shamed. This is particularly true when abuse happens or begins in childhood.

Feelings of rage. Rage almost always follows having been shamed. It serves a much-needed self-protective function of both insulating the self against further exposure and actively keeping others away.

Fear, hurt, distress, or rage can also accompany or follow shame experiences as secondary reactions. For example, feeling exposed is often followed by fear of further exposure and further occurrences of shame. Rage protects the self against further exposure. And along with shame, a victim can feel intense hurt and distress from having been abused.

The following exercise can help you discover what your primary feeling experiences of shame are.

Exercise: Your Feeling Experience of Shame

While you may have experienced all the feelings listed above, you may resonate with some more than others. Think about each type of abuse that you suffered and the various feelings that accompanied it. Ask yourself which of the items listed above stand out to you the most for each type of abuse, or each experience of abuse. In my case, for example, when I think about the sexual abuse I suffered at age nine, I resonate most profoundly with defectiveness, isolation, self-blame, and rage.

Further Defining Self-Compassion

If compassion is the ability to feel and connect with the suffering of another human being, self-compassion is the ability to feel and connect with one's own suffering. More specifically for our purposes, self-compassion is the act of extending compassion to one's self in instances of perceived inadequacy, failure, or general suffering. If we are to be self-compassionate, we need to give ourselves the recognition, validation, and support we would offer a loved one who is suffering.

Kristin Neff, a professor of psychology at the University of Texas at Austin, is the leading researcher in the growing field of self-compassion. In her book Self-Compassion (2011), she defines self-compassion as "being open to and moved by one's own suffering, experiencing feelings of caring and kindness toward oneself, taking an understanding, nonjudgmental attitude toward one's inadequacies and failures, and recognizing that one's experience is part of the common to ourselves with the same kindness, caring, and compassion we would show a good friend or a beloved child. Just as connecting with the suffering of others has been shown to comfort and heal, connecting with our own suffering will do the same. If you are able to feel compassion toward others, you can learn to feel it for yourself human experience" (224).

Self-compassion encourages us to begin to treat ourselves and talk; the following exercise will show you how.

Exercise: Becoming Compassionate Toward Yourself

1. Think about the most compassionate person you have known—someone kind, understanding, and supportive of you. It may have been a teacher, a friend, a friend's parent, a relative. Think about how this person conveyed his or her compassion toward you and how you felt in this person's presence.

Notice the feelings and sensations that come up with this memory. If you can't think of someone in your life who has been compassionate toward you, think of a compassionate public figure, or even a fictional character from a book, film, or television.

2. Now imagine that you have the ability to become as compassionate toward yourself as this person has been toward you (or you imagine this person would be toward you). How would you treat yourself if you were feeling overwhelmed with sadness or shame? What kinds of words would you use to talk to yourself?

This is the goal of self-compassion: to treat yourself the same way the most compassionate person you know would treat you—to talk to yourself in the same loving, kind, supportive ways this compassionate person would talk to you.

The Benefits of Practicing Self-Compassion

By learning to practice self-compassion you will also be able to begin doing the following:

- Truly acknowledge the pain you suffered and in so doing, begin to heal
- Take in compassion from others
- Reconnect with yourself, including reconnecting with your emotions
- Gain an understanding as to why you have acted out in negative and/or unhealthy ways
- Stop blaming yourself for your victimization
- Forgive yourself for the ways you attempted to cope with the abuse
- Learn to be deeply kind toward yourself
- Create a nurturing inner voice to replace your critical inner voice
- Reconnect with others and become less isolated

I hope I have been able to convey to you how self-compassion can help heal you of your shame. But it is difficult to adequately explain this concept in one blog. In the coming weeks I will write more blogs about how shame can be healed with self-compassion and explain to you how you can go about becoming more self-compassionate. As you continue reading the blogs and practicing the exercises you will grow to more fully understand what a powerful healer compassion can be.

In the next blog I will discuss the various obstacles that get in our way of becoming more self-compassionate including: our belief that self-compassion is the same as "feeling sorry for ourselves," the belief that self-compassion is selfish, and our need to forgive ourselves for past actions in order to believe we deserve self-compassion.

Originally published in Psychology Today, 2/28/17. Reprinted with permission.

A Breathing Exercise to Calm Panic Attacks

by David Carbonell, Ph.D.,

Here' a simple breathing exercise that will restore your comfortable breathing and soothe many of the physical symptoms of a panic attack. You may have already tried deep breathing and not had much success in soothing your panic symptoms. The reason for that is that most descriptions of deep breathing leave out a critical step. I'm going to show you how to do it right.

A simple, but powerful, technique

If you have Panic Disorder or Social Phobia, this deep breathing exercise may be the single most important coping technique I can show you. It's also useful with other anxiety disorders in which the physical symptoms are less prominent, but still present. Comfortable, deep breathing is the key to relaxation. All the traditional relaxation methods (yoga, meditation, hypnosis) place a central emphasis on breathing.

I can't catch my breath!

Feeling like "I can't catch my breath!" is probably the most common of all panic symptoms.

Your breathing feels labored, you strain to take a deep breath, you fear you're not going to get it—and the harder you try, the worse it feels!

When you feel short of breath, it doesn't mean you're not getting enough air. In fact, people will often say 'I can't catch my breath', and this shows that they're getting air, because we talk by making air vibrate. If you're talking, you're breathing! It's not a dangerous symptom. But it does get people very scared, and it produces other uncomfortable physical symptoms, so it's worth your while to be able to correct it.

You've probably already had it told to you, and you've probably also read it as well, that what you need to do is 'take a deep breath'. If you're like most people, that advice hasn't helped you much. It's good advice, but it's incomplete. It doesn't tell you how to take a deep breath. A good breathing exercise should tell you how to take a deep breath, and that's what I'm going to do.

Here's the Key

When you feel like you can't catch your breath, it's because you forgot to do something.

You forgot to exhale.

That's right. Before you can take a deep breath, you have to give one away. Why? Because, when you've been breathing in a short, shallow manner (from your chest), if you try and take a deep inhale, you just can't do it. All you can do is take a more labored, shallow breath from your chest. That will give you all the air you need, but it won't feel good.

Go ahead, try that now and see what I mean. Put one hand on your chest, the other on your belly. Breathe very shallowly from your chest a few times, then try to take a deep breath. I think you'll find that when you inhale you use your chest muscles, rather than your diaphragm, or belly. When you breathe is this shallow manner, you get all the air you need to live, but you can also get other symptoms which add to your panic.

You get chest pain or heaviness, because you've tightened the muscles of your chest to an uncomfortable degree. (The chest pain people feel in a panic attach isn't from the heart, it's from the muscles of the chest). You feel lightheaded or dizzy because shallow breathing can produce the same sensations as hyperventilation. You also get a more rapid heartbeat, and maybe numbness or tingling in the extremities as well.

All from breathing short and shallow!

One of the very first things I ask my patients with panic disorder to do is to learn and practice belly breathing. I recommend it to you as well. Here's the breathing exercise.

Belly Breathing Exercise

1. Place one hand just above your belt line, and the other on your chest, right over the breastbone. You can use your hands as a simple biofeedback device. Your hands will tell you what part of your body, and what muscles, you are using to breathe.

2. Open your mouth and gently sigh, as if someone had just told you something really annoying. As you do, let your shoulders and the muscles of your upper body relax, down, with the exhale. The point of the sigh is not to completely empty your lungs. It's just to relax the muscles of your upper body.

3. Close your mouth and pause for a few seconds.

4. Keep your mouth closed and inhale—slowly through your nose by pushing your stomach out. The movement of your stomach precedes the inhalation by just the tiniest fraction of a second, because it's this motion which is pulling the air in. When you've inhaled as much air as you can comfortably (without throwing your upper body into it), just stop. You're finished with that inhale.

5. Pause. How long? You decide. I'm not going to give you a specific count, because everybody counts at a different rate, and everybody has different size lungs. Pause briefly for whatever time feels comfortable. However, be aware that when you breathe this way, you are taking larger breaths than you're used to. For this reason, it's necessary to breathe more slowly than you're used to. If you breathe at the same rate you use with your small, shallow breaths, you will probably feel a little lightheaded from over breathing and it might make you yawn. Neither is harmful. They're just signals to slow down. Follow them!

6. Open your mouth. Exhale through your mouth by pulling your belly in.

7. Pause.

8. Continue with Steps 4-7.

NOW TRY THE BREATHING EXERCISE

If you've been struggling with panic for a while it's probably the opposite of how you usually breathe. That's because you've become a chest breather. You can live that way, but it will make it harder to overcome panic. Go ahead and practice the breathing exercise for a few minutes.

You may find it awkward at first, because it's very different than your present habit. But...all of us come into the world breathing this way. If you want to see some world class belly breathers, visit some newborns or infants!

Let Your Hands Be Your Guide!

Your hands will tell you if you're doing this correctly or not. Where is the muscular movement of the breathing? You want it to occur at your stomach; your upper body should be relatively still. If you feel movement in your chest, or notice your head and shoulders moving upwards, start again at Step 1, and practice getting the motion down to your stomach.

How did you do with the deep breathing practice?

You might have had some difficulty, because breathing in the short, shallow way is such an old habit for people who struggle with anxiety. Don't let that bother you. It just means you need persistent, patient practice. Breathing style is a habit, and the best way to retrain a habit is lots and lots of repetitions of the new habit.

Troubleshooting Tips

- If you have trouble redirecting your breathing from chest to stomach, practice isolating your stomach muscles first. Interlace your fingers across your stomach, and practice pushing your stomach out, then in, without breathing. As you get good at that, begin to pair it with your breathing.
- Use a variety of postures. When you're sitting down, you may find that leaning back in the chair, or leaning forward with your forearms on your thighs makes it a little easier than sitting up perfectly straight.

- Lie on your back. You can put a heavy book or other object on your chest to make it easier to focus on using your stomach muscles.
- Lie on your front, with a pillow beneath your stomach, and pressing your stomach against the pillow.
- Practice in front of a full-length mirror, to see what you are doing.
- If you are unable to breathe comfortably through your nose, due to allergies or any other reason, use your mouth instead. You will need to inhale even more slowly this way, in order to avoid gulping your air.

You'll know you've mastered this technique once your breathing feels more relaxing and soothing.

Build the Deep Breathing Habit

How often should you practice deep breathing? As often as possible, in sessions of one minute or so, for two weeks.

When it's time to practice, the first thing to do is notice how you've been breathing. Then switch to belly breathing for about one minute, as you continue doing whatever you were doing before you started. Don't interrupt your activity. You want good breathing to be portable!

How much is enough?

My patients usually want to know if they have to breathe this way all the time.

The answer is no.

Just focus on mastering the technique through regular brief practice. Add it to your list of first aid steps to take when you have a panic attack. Use it whenever you experience a strong, unpleasant emotion. Over time, I think you'll find that you use this kind of breathing more and more as you make it your new habit. But you can let that happen naturally just by following the suggestions above.

David Carbonell, Ph.D. is an anxiety coach. This article was originally published at www.anxietycoach.com. Reprinted with permission.

Writing Exercises For Self-Exploration

by Ben Colodzin Ph.D.

1. Instructions For How To Do Steppingstones

This is a writing method for self-exploration. It is inspired by and adapted from the work of a psychologist named Ira Progoff, who developed a lot of writing methods called the Intensive Journal Process. You can get his books or contact his organization to learn about his very useful methods.

I developed a set of instructions for self-exploratory writing that is easy to learn, that I have shared with many people who have found it useful. It can help to develop insight as to where you have been, how it has influenced your thinking and emotions, and conditioned you to behave in certain ways. When you use these methods, it is important to say first that you are writing just for YOU—you don't ever have to share what you write with anybody, ever. You may choose to do so, but that is completely up to you. This is really important because this only produces good effects if you tell the truth—and almost always people are better at telling themselves more of their personal truth than at sharing it with anybody else.

Okay, after making sure that the people you are teaching this to know that they don't have to share it with anybody, the next thing to describe is what exactly is a person supposed to be looking for, when they write their steppingstones? Because you are not looking for an historically accurate account of everything that happened in your life, this is not an autobiography where you have to get all the details correct. Instead, it is an exercise using your imagination, and seeing what comes up in your thoughts as you imagine in a very specific, structured way.

The point is NOT to remember everything that ever happened in one's life; instead, when you do this, you are actually interested in asking the question:

'What story do I tell myself, about my life?"

And the reason that is important is because we all tell ourselves only parts of the true story of our lives. The story you tell yourself about your life, also called personal mythology, is a mixture of real things that have happened, and also the ways you have been taught and conditioned to think. We all have to one degree or another what is called selective attention—which means we pay attention to some things and don't pay attention so well to other things. So some people remember only horrible things that have happened in their lives, and tell themselves a story that is filled with that; other people remember mostly the positive things that have happened, and tell themselves a story filled with that. Some people tell themselves a story where they are mostly a hero; others tell themselves a story where they are mostly a villain. And whatever story you tell yourself about who you are, colors how you think, what feelings are important to you, and how you act in the world. There is this thing they call self-fulfilling prophecy—that when you tell yourself that things are going to go a certain way, you tend to behave in ways that are preparing for that way to unfold—and by so doing you increase the chance that things really will go the way that is in line with your story about what will happen.

To give an example: there is this story about a guy who gets a flat tire in the middle of nowhere, in the middle of a cold, rainy night, and has to start walking towards town to get help because he has a spare tire, but no jack. And he has experienced lots of unhelpful people in his life, in his story people usually don't want to give him any assistance. So as he walks along, he begins to think of all the negative things that could happen when he knocks on the door of the first house he sees to use the phone: maybe he's going to wake up their infant son, and they'll be pissed off for that; or with his bad luck, maybe they'll have a vicious dog; or maybe there's been burglars in the area and they'll shoot when he knocks on the door late at night; or maybe they're just assholes who won't loan him their jack because they think he will steal it. So after a few miles walking and having thoughts pop into his head that come out of his personal mythology, he reaches a house and knocks on the door. A smiling woman answers and says "can I help you?" and he, caught up in his own story, replies "You can keep your goddamn jack!" and walks away.

A little corny, but a real example about how the story you tell yourself about yourself, can lead you to thinking about the world and what is going to happen in certain ways. And some of those ways can be self-defeating and self-sabotaging. So the idea here is to get information from the inside, from inside YOU, about the story you are telling yourself, about you. And to use that information to expand your ability to react in a wider variety of ways, because the truth is, we only tell ourselves parts of our story, the truth of our lives is always bigger than the story we tell ourselves about it.

So if you have any interest in changing behaviors, or figuring out how any negative thought patterns may have become stuck in your head, this can help to gain new information about how that is for you.

And it is also important to say that doing this isn't necessarily easy. Doing the exercise itself is pretty easy, but for people who have lived lives that hold real traumatic events, they can come up in the mind while doing this. And that can be triggering, stressful and difficult. So everybody has to do these kinds of things at their own pace, in their own time, without outside pressure telling them to do it a certain way and at a certain pace. That kind of outside pressure will screw it up. Because one of the major symptoms of post-traumatic stress is avoidance, avoiding thinking about or turning your attention towards anything that reminds you of the traumas. And in these exercises, you are going to be inviting yourself to search for things that made a difference, in shaping you as you are. And certainly for many people that includes very difficult traumas. So you have to be careful when doing this, to know when you are stressing out, to back off when it's feeling too hard to stay with it. You can get back to it in your own time, when you feel you can contain the stress reactions well enough that doing this doesn't knock you too far off balance.

So that is the basic explanation about why to try this at all. Now we'll move on to how to actually do the exercise, and then talk about how to use whatever comes up for you as you do it.

For the purpose of this exercise, I need to define what I mean when I say steppingstone. A steppingstone is defined like this

"Something that happened in my life, that made a difference in shaping me as I am"

A steppingstone can be anything, they can be good, bad, ugly, or neutral. The important quality of a steppingstone is that it had a real influence on you. They can be positive, negative, or contain elements of both. Could be a person that influenced you in some important way; or a book you read that made a real impact; a religious experience, a sexual experience, a nature experience, a traumatic experience—could be anything. Could be the first time you tasted a particular taste; or a particular idea came into your life; or a dream you have had. The ones that are steppingstones for YOU are the ones that made a difference, in shaping you as you are.

But the thing is, to say it again and again, when you are doing this exercise you are NOT trying to remember every historical detail of your life accurately, and then decide which ones are important enough to include as steppingstones. That would be using your conscious mind to analyze your life, and you've all probably done plenty of that already. Instead, you are going to be using your imagination, you are going to imagine and visualize a particular image, and see what pops up in your mind. Your job is not going to be to think about what comes up and analyze it; your job is to follow the specific instructions of imagining, and record what comes up in your mind when you do it. I will describe how to do that next.

First thing is to do this at a time when you won't be interrupted by distractions. Get physically comfortable as you can. Close your eyes and take a deep breath in, and let it out.

Then, you imagine yourself in some kind of place, in your mind's eye, some kind of place that feels safe to be, and that place is on high ground. It can be on a mountaintop, or a hilltop, on top of a tall building, or if you don't like heights it can just be on ground that is a few feet higher than the wide valley you will be looking at below you. Whatever high place you choose, you want to actually imagine it as best you can, what does it look like? Do this for as long as it takes to actually be able to imagine yourself on this high ground, looking down at some kind of valley below you.

You are standing on high ground, and as you look down at the valley below you, you notice that there is a road that goes through it. And that road is what we are imagining to be The Road Of Your Life. There is a place where you were born, and that is the starting point that we can see of this road. And the road stretches from there up until the present time, when you are here now. The road can look like anything: it might be a country road, might be a freeway, might be straight or curvy, might be sunny or rainy, it is up to your imagination to decide what the Road Of Your Life looks like. So now you are standing on high ground, in a place that is safe to be, and looking down on the road of your life.

And now you are beginning the Steppingstones process. You raise your binoculars (or any vision assisting eyewear if you don't like binoculars) to the first visible part of the road, and you say to yourself

"I was born (here) and then...."

And you begin to scan forward along the road, from that point where you were born, until something pops up in your mind. Something that happened, that made a difference in shaping you as you are. That is a steppingstone.

Now, in my personal life, the first time I did this, the first thing that popped up for me was when my family first got a dog, I was age four. We lived on the 5th floor of an apt building in New York, I was a city kid. And this dog was the first natural creature I got to know; he made a difference in my life. And his name was Mugsy. So when the thought of Mugsy popped into my mind, when I was scanning along the road of my life, I opened my eyes and wrote on my paper just one word that would remind me of that steppingstone—his name Mugsy. Because you don't want to find a steppingstone and then start explaining in lots of words why it is a steppingtone, all you are doing at this point when you are searching inside yourself is just imagining you are scanning along the road of your life, while imagining you are looking for things that made a difference. And so Mugsy came up in my head, I opened my eyes and wrote Mugsy, then I closed my eyes again and went back to my place on high ground, looking at my road. I went to that place on the road where Mugsy popped into my head, and continued scanning forward from there along the road, saying to myself "and then...." until I encountered another steppingstone. And then again, I wrote down a single word or two that reminded me of that steppingstone, and returned to the exercise until I had scanned to the present time.

Basically that is the exercise, to record what comes up, when you scan like that with your imagination, looking for the things that made a difference. And there's a few things I should say about that. How long do you do it for? No set amount of time. You can do it in three minutes, or take an hour. Up to you. Usually I suggest people try it for just five to ten minutes, and see what comes up. Not everything that is important will come up the first time, and that is okay. Remember, not trying to write your whole history, you are just asking yourself, "When I ask myself who I am, what do I tell myself?" These things that pop up along the road of your life are parts of what you tell yourself. Some of them you may tell yourself all the time; some of them may have been buried in your unconscious and you may not have consciously thought about them in a long time. No judgment about that at this point, you are just imagining going along the road of your life, and seeing what comes up, and making a record of it as you do.

Another thing that is good to say is that sometimes, even though you start where you were born and go forward along your road, that sometimes steppingstones don't pop into your mind in the actual order in which they happened in your real life. And that is okay too, you are doing 'long range reconnaissance patrol' to find out what pops up in your imagination as you ask about what made a difference. Don't try to get the whole story, just scan along the road and see what comes up. And remember, you can go back to it and add to it, you don't have to finish up the first time. And in fact, most people who do it more than once have different things come up, at different times. And that's all parts of your story, that you are gathering.

So really, that's all there is to the most basic steppingstones exercise. Starting to use the power of your imagination to unearth information from inside yourself. It's really different than studying with a teacher or reading a book or anything else from outside, because this is coming from YOU. So it is one way to use the laboratory of your own direct experience to learn things. And it's something you can do on your own without any help from anybody else, or violating your privacy in any way.

Okay, that's how you do the basic step, but once you've done it, what good is it? How do you use whatever you wrote in any way that is useful? Some people just come up with one or two steppingstones, some people find a lot of them. Neither is right or wrong, it's just information about what happens when you think and imagine this way. Some people remember mostly painful things, some people remember mostly positive things. Again, it's just information about what happens when you think and imagine this way. It is making you more aware of the story you tell yourself, about yourself.

I want to say this again, because it is important—you need to stay on your high ground, looking down on the road of your life, when you do this. You do NOT want to imagine walking along that road, and re living those times. Because if you do that if and when you hit traumatic moments, they can trigger you into feeling those hard feelings right now. You are just observing from a distance, and recording what comes up.

All right, suppose you have done this once or a few times, and you have some paper with some words on it that remind you of your steppingstones that you have remembered. What to do with it? Now you can begin to analyze what you have written. How many of those steppingstones have a positive quality or feel good to remember? How many are negative or feel bad to remember? That is already telling you something about the story you tell yourself. When you remember a particular steppingstone, does it have an emotional charge for you? Steppingstones can have either a negative or positive emotional charge, or they can be neutral. Any kind of reaction like 'ouch, I don't want to remember that' is what I mean by negative charge; any kind of reaction like 'yum, feels good when I remember that' is what I mean by positive charge; and ' I remember that happened and it did help shape me as I am but it doesn't really bring up any strong feelings in me one way or another when I remember it'. And when you look at your steppingstones and evaluate them in this way, you learn something about areas where you may be emotionally sensitive and areas where you may have some positive inner resources you can learn to draw upon. Another possible way to gain insight about the story you tell yourself, and its impact on you now.

That is the very first and most basic kind of analysis you can do with yourself. And when it comes to steppingstones that have a large emotional charge, you are being asked to just accept that when it comes to that particular steppingstone, there is still in the now a big emotional charge for you. Just notice that information in this inner laboratory of your direct experience.

You can apply it later on, if you learn the 'dialogues with the self' writing method.

If you locate any steppingstones that have a particularly good flavor for you, it feels good to remember it, then you can as an optional exercise take a blank paper and write down that steppingstone, then write 'it was a time when...' and write everything you can think of that was going on in that memory. The weather, what action was happening, what interested you. Sometimes you find positive images and behaviors that you can learn to import into your life now.

After you've done the most basic steppingstones, you can use the same method in more specific ways. First you do the steppingstones of your life; once you're comfortable with that, you can do the steppingstones of a specific aspect of your life. For example, you can do the steppingstones of your body. You would imagine putting a special filter on your binoculars or other eyepiece, so that it is only going to be seeing the things that made a difference in the life of your body. You would say to yourself, "my body was born, and then" ...and scan along the same road as before, looking only for things that made a difference in the life of your physical body.

If you're interested in relationships, you can put that filter on your eyepiece, and say "my relationships were born, and then..."and you will just be imagining things that happened in your relationships, that made a difference, and scan with that in mind. Same with sexual experiences— "my sex life was born, and then". Or "my military life was born, and then". You can put on any filter that interests you, any area of your life you want to examine, and use this imagination exercise, and write down what comes up. When you do this, your conscious mind is choosing to invite parts of your memory to surface and speak to you now. You can gather a whole lot of information that helps answer the question "When I ask myself who I am, what do I tell myself?" in this way.

2. Instructions for Dialogues With the Self

This is a more advanced method of digging deeper with the search inside yourself. It is more complicated to learn than the steppingstones method. And it needs some explanation to describe the ways that people have found it to be useful.

This is another way to use your imagination with a structured writing style to get more answers to the question "when I ask myself who am I, what do I tell myself?". When you use it, it is important to remember that really you are the only one creating the dialogue. Sometimes people use this method to have dialogues between themselves and someone else who has been important in their lives, and the dialogue produces a great result, and they become excited that they reached a new place with that person they had the dialogue with. But in reality they only reached that new place inside themselves, the real-life other person has no idea that you did this, or what insights or new perspective you may have reached. So you have to be careful when you use this exercise, and imagine speaking with other people who matter in your lives, to remember that even though you are imagining talking with other people, that really this is strictly you talking with yourself, this is dialogues with the self.

These kinds of dialogues can give you great insights and might help you find the words that are in your heart to speak to someone else, and that might really help prepare you to actually speak to that person, and maybe not, but this is just for yourself, like the steppingstones. This is to help you find out what you might want to say to that other person, or even to some part of yourself, knowing what you know in your life now, if you had the chance to speak it to them now. And you can do this with people who are alive now and with people who are not, it's your imagination, and you can exercise it however you choose.

You can also have dialogues that aren't with another person, that are with a part of yourself. Like, for example, if you've ever been addicted to anything, you can have a dialogue with the part of you that's hungry for whatever you're hungry for. Or used to be hungry for. You can have a dialogue with your male sex organ, what gets joked about as the 'little brain'. You know that joke, why do men have a hole in the end of their penis? To get oxygen to the brain. You can have a dialogue and let the big brain and the little brain talk things over. So there's a lot of ways you can apply this imagination exercise.

Mostly I have shared this stuff where people want to reduce some of the emotional charge out of what happens when they have trauma-related stress reactions. And for that purpose, I explain this idea of 'unfinished business' as I call it. When you did your basic steppingstones, I asked you to notice when looking at them later to notice if any of them had a positive/negative/or neutral emotional charge. Do you remember that? Did you do it? If not, go back and do that now, it is part of the preparation to be ready to get into this next method.

Okay. If you noticed any difference in the emotional charge you felt, when looking at your various steppingstones, good. That is you using your 'felt sense', the sensing system inside yourself. When you are the chief investigator, psychologist, judge and jury, and healer, using your 'felt sense' as a measuring tool inside the laboratory of your own inner world is important. You want to sensitize yourself to these kinds of feelings, which really means to become aware of them.

When you looked at your steppingstones, and things that happened that made a difference in shaping you as you are, did any of them evoke inside you a strong emotional reaction? It can be a positive or negative emotional reaction, here you are just measuring the intensity of your reaction, both the most horrible thing that once happened and the most amazingly good thing that once happened could both produce strong reactions. And if they do, that is a clue you are receiving from your inner sensing system, there is something there with which you have what I call 'unfinished business'. You're getting a blip on your inner radar, that this steppingstone still has some kind of important meaning for you. Some kind of energy is bound up there, so that when it gets tweaked by remembering it, you somehow get stimulated by that 'old business' and start reacting to it, some pattern that got imprinted on you back then is running again now, that is why I call it 'unfinished business'.

And finding ways to deal with 'unfinished business', does not mean just going back into old painful situations and reliving them, that is not the idea here. Instead this method asks you to be where you are in your life now, as a person who knows that steppingstone is part of what has happened in your life. And from that place, as you are now, speaking from all you have learned up to where you are now, to speak what was not spoken before, that is in your heart to speak.

Many people have told me this has produced good things for them. Shifts in point of view. Ability to mourn and grieve things they were avoiding for a long time. Insights about why things went the ways they did. And some amazement, that something so useful could actually come out of themselves, on their own, after all this time feeling stuck in old patterns.

When I first started teaching here, I heard about this program at San Quentin, they called it

Healing from the Inside Out, it was some kind of writing program run by incarcerated vets there, I tried to make a connection with them and facilitate communication between their group and what I was trying to do here. That didn't work, but I know they were on the same track, the same idea I am trying to promote here. And that is that it is not about me or them or any particular group or copyrighted method of treatment. That's all ego and merchandising. People have some power to learn about themselves, from the inside out. In an environment like this the very best thing I can do for you is to help you remember that applies to you too.

Okay, back to 'unfinished business'. Where there is a big emotional charge, there may well be some unfinished business. If the emotional charge is negative and produces pts-like reactions, there is a really good chance you've got some unfinished business there. If the emotional charge is positive and produces a softening in your heart, or anything else that you would consider more warm and fuzzy than usual, there may or may not be unfinished business, there could be other clues from your 'felt sense' about what it takes to get you feeling warm and fuzzy more often.

Dialogues with your most positive steppingstones can enable gratitude and thanksgiving. Remembering and giving respect to whatever is still good, despite all that isn't. Which is relaxing and can help soften up alienation and depression. At least that is my point of view.

Dialogues with your most negative steppingstones can be painful. Don't try this the first time with your mostly highly charged negative places. Get

213

used to how to do it before you go near the touchiest places.

I don't present this as a miraculous cure. Engaging like this can stress you, can bring up anger, or can evoke sadness and mourning and grieving. Often with traumatic histories people didn't have time back then to allow themselves to feel all the feelings that traumas bring up, and some kind of energetic impact from back then may still be bottled up inside. These kind of dialogues between the you who is alive now, and what he would say to whoever you have the unfinished business with if they were right here right now, can be really intense, this is deep level trauma work. And people often tell me, they have avoided these painful memories for years, why should they bring them up now? Won't that do more harm than good?

And I tell them, I am NOT asking you to go out and look for difficult memories, or go anywhere inside yourself you are not ready to go. I am just asking you to look at the road of your life, and see what comes up. If that stuff comes up now, I am asking you to accept the fact that whatever came up is here in your now, it's part of what you are noticing now, part of the story you are telling yourself about who you are, as something that helped shape who you are, it's not just in the past for you but also in the present. So I am inviting you to use all that you have learned since back then, all that you have added to the story of who you are, and from that place now, to speak your wisdom gleaned from your life, to whoever and whatever places you have unfinished business according to your inner 'felt sense'.

And if there are traumatic events that made a difference in shaping you as you are, as has been the case for almost everybody I have met here at CTF, and if during those times you didn't have time or space to mourn and grieve the losses that happened then, as has also been the case for almost everybody I have met here, then very possibly there is some kind of energy bound up inside you. And finding healthy ways to release and discharge some of that energy during triggering events helps people feel more self-control and ability to maintain mental, physical, and emotional balance.

Elizabeth Kubler-Ross once described various stages a person goes through when they realize they are dying. These stages can also apply to the losses that come with traumatic events.

They begin with the stage of denial (it's not happening). Then the stage of bargaining or minimizing (okay, something is happening, but it isn't that serious). Then the stage of anger (I know it's happening, and I'm really pissed off about it). Then grieving (I know it's happening, and I'm so sad to experience it). And finally acceptance (I know it's happening; I have processed my feelings about it and I accept it is so). And these stages or ways of dealing can happen in any sequence or combination. But often for people who don't get a chance to process mourning and grieving after overwhelming events, behavior patterns develop that can get stuck in anger as a way of expressing what the felt sense is feeling. So why am I saying all this? Because giving yourself permission to have dialogues with unfinished business can be a powerful tool to help you learn where there may be hidden mourning and grieving work you need to do to address some of your unfinished business. And if you do that, you can start unlocking some of your behavior programs, from the inside out. You can get clues and develop insights that change your perspective and help you be stuck in anger less often. Do I know that is going to happen for every guy that tries this? Of course not. But some of the guys here that have done this have said to me that it helped them do those things, or I wouldn't say that.

I'm not saying that you may not have plenty of valid things to get angry about, I don't want to take away your right to feel anger. I just want people to get a better handle on old hair trigger reflexes. I like this story a friend told me, that he had heard the Tibetan Dalai Lama get asked the question, why didn't he stay in Tibet and fight against the Chinese invasion? And he answered that he didn't choose to stay and fight, because if he engaged in the war, 'then the war would be inside me'. And so it can be with overwhelming traumas, they get inhaled through our experience, and they affect us, they leave their imprints. The war from those traumatic events gets inside us. And that certainly can include anger, rage, depression, all of that. The trauma got inhaled, and somehow it is inside you. The more you can do to make peace with its presence, with how things really are for you, the more skillful you can become at keeping your balance when stress reactions do come up.

I remember this story that got told in a PTSD documentary the Veterans

Administration put out about 25 years ago. It featured this Marine combat vet, and he was talking about how he had learned to control his conditioned responses. He said that after he returned to civilian life, he found that when he was driving in traffic and somebody cut him off in an unsafe driving maneuver, he immediately felt like that person was trying to kill him, to put his life at risk, he wanted to get out of his car and attack that person, he was in such a rageful state. And the guy talking had done a bunch of therapy, he had gone thru various methods to realize that he needed to modify his thinking about the appropriate response to various kinds of threats. And he said in this documentary "now when somebody cuts me off while driving, I don't think about beating the shit of them anymore. I just flip them off." His audience laughed when he said that, and he remained serious and said "that may sound funny to you, but I am serious. Learning how to take the time to really check out the situation before I react has been life saving for me". And that is an example of the trajectory of PTSD stress reactivity recovery, learning how to gauge when it really is necessary to use combat trained responses and when to contain those impulses.

So that's some of the background for why do this dialogues thing, what is the point of it? That's the sales pitch. The reason is to get more of the story of who you are, what you tell yourself about who you are, and use that information to apply in your life now. And now to actually do it, this takes a few steps to go through.

Before beginning, same as all these imagination exercises, pick a time when you won't be interrupted, and make yourself comfortable.

Step One

The first step is to pick someone you want to have a dialogue with. You can pick anybody, but for the purposes of pts self-help recovery, I am suggesting you pick someone with whom you believe that you have unfinished business. Might be easiest to pick some unfinished business that has a positive charge, but that is up to you. Maybe somebody did something good that made a difference, and you never got a chance to say thanks. Or you can pick a negatively charged happening where you did something you now regret that you didn't feel sorry about at the time, and want to say how your perspective has changed. Up to you. But Step One is pick a definite person that you have some unfinished business with.

Step Two

Next step is to write one word or sentence—only one sentence—that describes the unfinished business. So, if you're writing to your mother you might write 'the way she treated me'. But whoever you choose, make sure you really specifically write one sentence describing in a general way what the unfinished business is about. Write that down at the top of the page, that's Step Two.

Step Three

Next step is a little weird, but your imagination can handle it. You are now going to do the Steppingstones of the person you are going to have the dialogue with. You are going to do the same exercise you did when you do the basic steppingstones, standing on high ground and looking at the road in the lower ground before you, only this time you will be looking at the road of somebody else's life. The other person in your dialogue.

Now of course you only know some of that person's history, much less than about yourself, and maybe you don't really know hardly anything about the things that made a difference in shaping that person into the person you knew. But that doesn't matter, because just like when you did your own steppingstones, you are not trying to get an accurate history of everything. You are just seeing what pops up in your mind when you exercise YOUR imagination in this way. If my dialogue is with John Doe, I would be standing up on my high ground and saying to myself

"John Doe was born, and then…." And scan along the road of his life that I am imagining, and see what pops up.

Now, sometimes you will have a person that made a difference, that you want to have a dialogue with, that you only knew for 10 minutes. But something important happened in that ten minutes. So if you only knew John Doe for 10 minutes, then you would just see what pops into your head during the parts of the road of his life that you know about. Maybe something will come up, maybe nothing. And that is okay either way. The important thing in this step is that you are tuning your imagination to thinking about John Doe, getting yourself ready to have a dialogue with him. So you just spend a couple of minutes, or longer if you wish, scanning along the road of John Doe's life, writing down whatever pops into your head when you think of anything that made a difference, in who he is or was. That's Step Three.

Step Four

Now you are ready for Step Four, where you actually begin to imagine starting a conversation.

Keeping in mind the one sentence you wrote down about the unfinished business between you and your chosen John or Jane Doe, you close your eyes and imagine yourself sitting somewhere, comfortably. And in the room with you, a safe and comfortable distance away, John or Jane Doe is sitting in another chair. Imagine they are here now, and you can look at them. While you are remembering the unfinished business, and while you are imagining they are somehow here right now with the you who is alive now and is the holder of all the knowledge you have gained in this life, you imagine looking in their eyes and speak what you would really actually say to them, about the unfinished business, if they were here now.

And you open your eyes and write that down, doing all that is Step Four. And how you begin the conversation. ...that's totally up to you, see what comes up inside when you imagine that way. And whatever comes up, don't edit it or think if that is right or wrong, just allow it to be there,. Write it down. It might be as simple as 'hi', or 'you ready to talk?' or it might launch in any direction. No right or wrong to it. Just notice what you imagine you really would say if it were happening right now, and write that down.

Step Five

The next step is really the trickiest part of this whole thing. You see, when you're doing this, you are imagining there is a conversation going on. And in your imagination, you are one of the two people having the conversation. So when it's your turn to talk, you just imagine yourself sitting there with the other person, saying whatever you have to say. But after you do that, you have to do something different. You do not want to think up the answer that you believe the other person would give, you do not want to say to yourself "well, I know if I said this, they would say that". You just want to go into this receptive place, quiet your thoughts as much as you can while you imagine yourself looking at that other person, after you spoke whatever you said to them. And see what comes up as you look at them, see what pops up for you. Maybe they don't answer at all, but have some kind of body language, they smile, or frown, or flip you off, or whatever they do. Whatever you saw them do or imagined they spoke to you, you write that down. That's the next step.

Step Six

So now you have followed your imagination this far, you have imagined you were speaking to this other person right now about some particular unfinished business, and you found some words to speak, then you just watched and listened for a little while and wrote down whatever popped up in your imagination about how they responded to you. Just let yourself receive whatever 'they' say, and let that settle in for a bit.

You imagine you are really there with them, and you said what you said, and then they said or did what they said or did. Well, if they really responded to you in that way, right now after you spoke to them, how would you respond to their response? What pops up in you that you would say next? Whatever comes up, write that down. That's the next step.

Step Seven

Then, again, you go back to that receptive mode, after you say your piece, you imagine watching and listening to that other person again, see what comes up in your imagination as their next response. You keep going with this, back and forth in this way, for as long as it seems there is something to say. Sometimes it doesn't seem to go anywhere; sometimes it's one or two sentences and that's it; sometimes it takes on a life of its own and it goes on for pages and pages. It's your imagination, and your free choice how you do and don't want to direct it. That is the basic way that the dialogues with the self method can work, to assist in 'long range reconnaissance patrol' inside one's self and help you learn about and process the ways you relate to unfinished business.

This is a powerful tool and I certainly recommend that it be treated carefully and with respect. As humans we all have some light and some darkness inside us, and this can bring attention to both. If you find inner places you do not want to go near, that is okay and to be respected. You may not be ready to handle emotionally charged stimuli without losing your balance and acting out. You have to develop honest self appraisal of your skill level in maintaining balance or 'holding your seat' as it is also called. If you are in a place where you lose control when you remember traumatic events, you may not be ready to use this kind of method. I recommend that when it comes to big traumas and history that has been avoided and repressed for a long time, it's usually necessary to learn some stress reduction and anger management tools, and develop some skill and confidence in using them when you have intense stress reactions, to help you learn to hold your balance, and contain your emotions within yourself as reactions come up in you. And they will, sometimes, that is kind of predictable. If there are old emotional poisons hidden inside, it's kind of like going to the dentist, not where you go for fun, but a place you need to go get some stuff cleaned up if you don't want the poisons to hurt you even worse. This method is not some miraculous cure or anything like that. It's just an easy to use doorway into your own imagination, what you get out of it mostly depends on what you put into it. My prayer and my intention in sharing it with you is that it be applied usefully to help ease suffering and bring clarity to those who are asking for these things.

Meditation

by Richard Ranta

Here you are in prison. Now what do you do? How do you act? Who do you turn to for help? How do you get anything done? How do you get packages, appliances, such as a TV, radio, CDplayer, fan, etc.? Where are the groups? Where is the chow hall? How do you get to the yard? Who can I talk to or hang out with? These questions, and just being in prison for the first time, can lead you to a big headache and lots of stress. You will meet people who won't help you, talk to you, or will cause problems with you. Even your cellie, if you have one, can be a pain in the ass and can make your life miserable. Prison life can be a living hell if you don't know how to deal with it in the right way.

What do you do? What do you want to do? A lot of people will deal with it in a negative way. They usually end up in a fight or some kind of altercation with another individual. This will cause you even more problems. You will be written up and sent to the hole (Administrative Segregation), lose some or all of your privileges (going to the yard, being able to go the canteen, quarterly packages, special purchases, and even being able to come out of your cell for dayroom). Life can get out of hand really quickly if you are not paying attention to it to what you say or do.

How Are You Going To Deal With Everything?

One of the ways I have found to be helpful is meditation. It might sound like some way-out thing for most people, but it really does work if you are using it properly. It took me over 15 years of being in prison getting pissed off at the program, how things were done, how they ran the yard, getting locked down for something I had nothing to do with, and even getting mad about what we were served in the chow hall.

I was invited to a mindfulness group with some Vietnam Veterans, who saw how stressed out I was; and they wanted to help me. I was, to say the least, kind of skeptical. It took some months for me to be able to get to the point where I could totally relax; I found it to be very fulfilling. I started to notice a change in my attitude about things, the daily goings-on of the prison, to be less stressful than they had been in the past. I found restraint in situations, where in the past I had blown a gasket, to be easier to deal with. Prison life started to change for the better. My life and demeanor were calmer and more in control. I became a more positive person. I was able to handle stressful situations with less or no stress on my part. I found myself being able to do more and accomplish things I hadn't been able to do in the past. Life was getting good!

It took me some time to realize that it was the meditation that had helped me. It was something that you could do without doing anything. All I had to do was to just sit there, not think about anything but my breath. I started to be more outgoing, participated in more groups, even becoming a facilitator in a couple of them. I had never been able to do that before I started to do meditation. The biggest thing that I noticed was that I got along with others better. I wasn't an asshole all the time as in the past. My life improved and I was able to accomplish more. The tasks that I had a hard time dealing with before and were stressful to me were finished without me getting upset.

I can only let you know what I experienced from participating in meditation. You will have to make up your own mind. Those that I have shared my experience with, some have started meditating and found it to be helpful to them. Some don't think it will do any good for them. You be the judge. Give it a chance, not just a half-ass attempt, a real try. You just might be surprised what it can do for you and the way you see the world and everything in it!

Incarceration Syndrome

by Ron Self

This summary will provide a brief description of Incarceration Syndrome, describe some common symptoms, as well as review some self-management exercises.

Incarceration Syndrome is a set of symptoms that are present in many presently incarcerated, and recently released prisoners who have experienced physical or emotional abuse and have been subjected to prolonged incarceration in environments of punishment with few opportunities for education, vocational training, and self-help programming / rehabilitation efforts. The symptoms are most severe in prisoners who have been subjected to prolonged periods of solitary confinement and who have witnessed severe institutional abuse.

The severity of symptoms is directly related to the level of coping skills prior to incarceration, length of incarceration, the restrictiveness of the incarceration environment, the severity of institutional abuse episodes experienced, the degree of involvement in self-help programming, education, vocational and rehabilitation programs.

Symptoms of Incarceration Syndrome:

Institutional Personality Traits are brought about by living in an oppressive environment that demands:

- Passive compliance to demands of authority figures.
- Passive acceptance of severely restricted acts of daily living.
- Repression of personal lifestyle preferences.

- Reduction of critical thinking and individual decision making.
- Internalized acceptance of severe restrictions on the honest Self-expression of thoughts and feelings.

These symptoms are identical to what a front-line soldier or marine experiences on the battlefield.

Post Traumatic Stress Disorder:

From both traumatic experiences before incarceration and institutional abuse during incarceration that includes six clusters of symptoms:

- Intrusive memories and flashbacks of episodes of severe institutional abuse.
- Intense psychological distress and psychological reactivity when exposed to cues triggering memories of institutional abuse.
- Episodes of dissociation, emotional numbing, restrictive affect.
- Chronic problem with mental functioning that include irritability.
- Outburst of anger, difficulty concentrating, sleep disturbances, and exaggerated startle response.
- Persistent avoidance of anything that would trigger memories of the Traumatic events.
- Hypervigilance, generalized paranoia, and reduced capacity to trust caused by constant fear of abuse from both correctional staff and other inmates that can be generalized to others after release.

Antisocial Personality Traits:

Antisocial Personality Traits both preexisting and developed within the institution as an institutional coping skill and psychological defense mechanism.

The primary antisocial personality traits involve the tendency to challenge authority, break rules and victimize others. In clients with (I.S.) these tendencies are veiled by the passive aggressive style that is part of the institutional personality. Clients with (I.S.) tend to be duplicitous, acting in compliant and passive aggressive manner with perceived authority figures while being capable of direct threatening and aggressive behavior when alone with peers outside of the control of those in authority. This is a direct result of the internalized coping behavior required to survive in a harshly punitive correctional institution that has two sets of survival rules: passive aggressive with guards, and actively aggressive with other inmates.

Social-Sensory Deprivation Syndrome: Is caused by the effects of prolonged solitary confinement that imposed both social isolation and sensory deprivation. These symptoms include chronic headaches, developmental regression, impaired impulse control, dissociation, inability to anticipate logical consequences of behavior, out of control thinking and borderline personality traits.

This syndrome is most severe in prisoners incarcerated for longer than one year in a punishment-oriented environment, who have experienced multiple episodes of institutional abuse, who have little access to education, vocational training, self-help and/or rehabilitation.

The syndrome is least severe in prisoners incarcerated for shorter periods of time in rehabilitation-oriented programs, who have reasonable access to educational training, and who have not been subjected to solitary confinement, and who have not experienced frequent or severe episodes of institutional abuse.

Prisoners with (I.S.) are at high risk of developing substance dependence, relapsing to substance use if they were previously addicted and returning to a life of aggression, violence and crime.

They are also at high risk of unemployment and homelessness.

This is because released prisoners experiencing (I.S.) tend to experience a six-stage post release symptom progression leading to recidivism and often are not qualified for social benefits needed to secure addiction, mental health and occupational training services.

Stage 1

Helplessness and hopelessness due to inability to develop a plan for community re-entry, often complicated by the inability to secure funding for treatment or job training.

Stage 2

Intense immobilizing fear.

Stage 3

Emergence of intense free-floating anger and rage and the emergence of flashbacks and other symptoms of PTSD.

Stage 4

Tendency toward impulsive violence upon minimal provocation.

Stage 5

Effort to avoid violence by severe isolation to avoid the triggers of violence.

Stage 6

Intensification of flashbacks, nightmares, sleep impairments, and impulse control problems, caused by self-imposed isolation. This leads to acting out behaviors, aggression, violence, and crime, which in turn sets the stages for arrest, incarceration, and Domestic violence.

Incarceration syndrome presents identical to PTSD among combat veterans, and those who grew up in an urban environment.

This is an excerpt from an article that was originally published by Veterans Healing Veterans From the Inside Out (https://veteranshealingveterans.com). Reprinted with permission.

Post Incarceration Syndrome and Relapse (PICS)

by Terence Gorski

The Post Incarceration Syndrome (PICS) is a serious problem that contributes to relapse in addicted and mentally ill offenders who are released from correctional institutions.

Currently 60% of prisoners have been in prison before and there is growing evidence that the Post Incarceration Syndrome (PICS) is a contributing factor to this high rate of recidivism.[i]

The concept of a post incarceration syndrome (PICS) has emerged from clinical consultation work with criminal justice system rehabilitation programs working with currently incarcerated prisoners and with addiction treatment programs and community mental health centers working with recently released prisoners.

This article will provide an operational definition of the Post Incarceration Syndrome (PICS), describe the common symptoms, recommend approaches to diagnosis and treatment, explore the implications of this serious new syndrome for community safety, and discuss the need for political action to reduce the number of prisoners and assure more humane treatment within our prisons, jails, and correctional institutions as a means of prevention. It is my hope that this initial formulation of a PICS Syndrome will encourage researchers to develop objective testing tools and formal studies to add to our understanding of the problems encountered by released inmates that influence recovery and relapse.

Post Incarceration Syndrome (PICS) - Operational Definition

The Post Incarceration Syndrome (PICS) is a set of symptoms that are present in many currently incarcerated and recently released prisoners that are caused by being subjected to prolonged incarceration in environments of punishment with few opportunities for education, job training, or rehabilitation. The symptoms are most severe in prisoners subjected to prolonged solitary confinement and severe institutional abuse.

The severity of symptoms is related to the level of coping skills prior to incarceration, the length of incarceration, the restrictiveness of the incarceration environment, the number and severity of institutional episodes of abuse, the number and duration of episodes of solitary confinement, and the degree of involvement in educational, vocational, and rehabilitation programs.

The Post Incarceration Syndrome (PICS) is a mixed mental disorder with five clusters of symptoms:

(1) Institutionalized Personality Traits resulting from the common deprivations of incarceration, a chronic state of learned helplessness in the face of prison authorities, and antisocial defenses in dealing with a predatory inmate milieu, (2) Post Traumatic Stress Disorder (PTSD) from both pre-incarceration trauma and trauma experienced within the institution,

(3) Antisocial Personality Traits (ASPT) developed as a coping response to institutional abuse and a predatory prisoner milieu, and

(4) Social-Sensory Deprivation Syndrome caused by prolonged exposure to solitary confinement that radically restricts social contact and sensory stimulation.

(5) Substance Use Disorders caused by the use of alcohol and other drugs to manage or escape the PICS symptoms.

PICS often coexists with substance use disorders and a variety of affective and personality disorders.

Symptoms of the Post Incarceration Syndrome (PICS)

Below is a more detailed description of five clusters of symptoms of Post Incarceration Syndrome (PICS):

1. Institutionalized Personality Traits

Institutionalized Personality Traits are caused by living in an oppressive environment that demands: passive compliance to the demands of authority figures, passive acceptance of severely restricted acts of daily living, the repression of personal lifestyle preferences, the elimination of critical thinking and individual decision making, and internalized acceptance of severe restrictions on the honest self-expression thoughts and feelings.

2. Post-Traumatic Stress Disorder (PTSD)

Post-Traumatic Stress Disorder (PTSD) [ii] is caused by both traumatic experiences before incarceration and institutional abuse during incarceration that includes the six clusters of symptoms:

(1) intrusive memories and flashbacks to episodes of severe institutional abuse;

(2) intense psychological distress and physiological reactivity when exposed to cues triggering memories of the institutional abuse;

(3) episodes of dissociation, emotional numbing, and restricted affect;

(4) chronic problems with mental functioning that include irritability, outbursts of anger, difficulty concentrating, sleep disturbances, and an exaggerated startle response.

(5) persistent avoidance of anything that would trigger memories of the traumatic events;

(6) hypervigilance, generalized paranoia, and reduced capacity to trust caused by constant fear of abuse from both correctional staff and other inmates that can be generalized to others after release.

3. Antisocial Personality Traits

Antisocial Personality Traits [iii] [iv] [v] are developed both from preexisting symptoms and symptoms developed during incarceration as an institutional coping skill and psychological defense mechanism. The primary antisocial personality traits involve the tendency to challenge authority, break rules, and victimize others. In patients with PICS these tendencies are veiled by the passive aggressive style that is part of the institutionalized personality. Patients with PICS tend to be duplicitous, acting in a compliant and passive aggressive manner with therapists and other perceived authority figures while being capable of direct threatening and aggressive behavior when alone with peers outside of the perceived control of those in authority. This is a direct result of the internalized coping behavior required to survive in a harshly punitive correctional institution that has two set of survival rules: passive aggression with the guards, and actively aggressive with predatory inmates.

4. Social-Sensory Deprivation Syndrome:

The Social-Sensory Deprivation Syndrome [vi] is caused by the effects of prolonged solitary confinement that imposes both social isolation and sensory deprivation. These symptoms include severe chronic headaches, developmental regression, impaired impulse control, dissociation, inability to concentrate, repressed rage, inability to control primitive drives and instincts, inability to plan beyond the moment, inability to anticipate logical consequences of behavior, out of control obsessive thinking, and borderline personality traits.

5. Reactive Substance Use Disorders

Many inmates who experience PICS suffer from the symptoms of substance use disorders [vii]. Many of these inmates were addicted prior to incarceration, did not receive treatment during their imprisonment, and continued their addiction by securing drugs on the prison black market. Others developed their addiction in prison in an effort to cope with the PICS symptoms and the conditions causing them. Others relapse to substance abuse or develop substance use disorders as a result of using alcohol or other drugs in an effort to cope with PICS symptoms upon release from prison.

PICS Symptoms Severity

The syndrome is most severe in prisoners incarcerated for longer than one year in a punishment oriented environment, who have experienced multiple episodes of institutional abuse, who have had little or no access to education, vocational training, or rehabilitation, who have been subjected to 30 days or longer in solitary confinement, and who have experienced frequent and severe episodes of trauma as a result of institutional abuse.

The syndrome is least severe in prisoners incarcerated for shorter periods of time in rehabilitation-oriented programs, who have reasonable access to educational and vocational training, and who have not been subjected to solitary confinement, and who have not experienced frequent or severe episodes of institutional abuse.

Reasons To Be Concerned About PICS

There is good reason to be concerned because about 40% of the total incarcerated population (currently 700,000 prisoners and growing) are released each year. The number of prisoners being deprived of rehabilitation services, experiencing severely restrictive daily routines, being held in solitary confinement for prolonged periods of time, or being abused by other inmates or correctional staff is increasing. [viii]

The effect of releasing this number of prisoners with psychiatric damage from prolonged incarceration can have a number of devastating impacts upon American society including the further devastation of inner city communities and the destabilization of blue-collar and middle class districts unable to reabsorb returning prisoners who are less likely to get jobs, more likely to commit crimes, more likely to disrupt families. This could turn many currently struggling lower middle-class areas into slums. [ix]

As more prisoners are returned to the community, behavioral health providers can expect to see increases in patients admitted with the Post Incarceration Syndrome and related substance use, mental, and personality disorders. The national network of Community Mental health and Addiction treatment Programs need to begin now to prepare their staff to identify and provide appropriate treatment for this new type of client.

The nation's treatment providers, especially addiction treatment programs and community mental health centers, are already experiencing a growing number of clients experiencing the Post Incarceration Syndrome (PICS). This increase is due to a number of factors including: the increasing size of the prisoner population, the increasing use of restrictive and punishing institutional practices, the reduction of access to education, vocational training, and rehabilitation programs; the increasing use of solitary confinement and the growing number of maximum security and super-max type prison and jails.

Both the number of clients suffering from PICS and the average severity of symptoms is expected to increase over the next decade. In 1995 there were 463,284 prisoners released back to the community. Based upon conservative projections in the growth of the prisoner population it is projected that in the year 2000 there will be 660,000 prisoners returned to the community, in the year 2005 there will 887,000 prisoners returned to the community, and in the year 2010 1.2 million prisoners will be released.[x] The prediction of greater symptom severity is based upon the growing trend toward longer periods of incarceration, more restrictive and punitive conditions in correctional institutions, decreasing access to education, vocational training, and rehabilitation, and the increasing use solitary confinement as a tool for reducing the cost of prisoner management.

Clients with PICS are at a high risk for developing substance dependence, relapsing to substance use if they were previously addicted, relapsing to active mental illness if they were previously mentally ill, and returning to a life of aggression, violence, and crime.

They are also at high risk of chronic unemployment and homelessness.

Post Release Symptom Progression

This is because released prisoners experiencing PICS tend to experience a six-stage post release symptom progression leading to recidivism and often are not qualified for social benefits needed to secure addiction, mental health, and occupation training services.

- Stage 1 of this Post Release Syndrome is marked by Helplessness and hopelessness due to inability to develop a plan for community reentry, often complicated by the inability to secure funding for treatment or job training;
- Stage 2 is marked by an intense immobilizing fear;
- Stage 3 is marked by the emergence of intense free-floating anger and rage and the emergence of flashbacks and other symptoms of PTSD;
- Stage 4 is marked by a tendency toward impulse violence upon minimal provocation;
- Stage 5 is marked by an effort to avoid violence by severe isolation to avoid the triggers of violence;
- Stage 6 is marked by the intensification of flashbacks, nightmares, sleep impairments, and impulse control problems caused by self-imposed isolation. This leads to acting out behaviors, aggression, violence, and crime, which in turn sets the stages for arrest and incarceration.

Currently 60% of prisoners have been in prison before and there is growing evidence that the Post Incarceration Syndrome (PICS) is a contributing factor to this high rate of recidivism.

Reducing The Incidence Of PICS

Since PICS is created by criminal justice system policy and programming in our well-intentioned but misguided attempt to stop crime, the epidemic can be prevented and public safety protected by changing the public policies that call for incarcerating more people, for longer periods of time, for less severe offenses, in more punitive environments that emphasize the use of solitary confinement, that eliminate or severely restrict prisoner access to educational, vocational, and rehabilitation programs while incarcerated.

The political antidote for PICS is to implement public policies that:

(1) Fund the training and expansion of community-based addiction and mental health programs staffed by professionals trained to meet the needs of criminal justice system clients diverted into treatment by court programs and released back to the community after incarceration;

(2) Expand the role of drug and mental health courts that promote treatment alternatives to incarceration;

(3) Convert 80% of our federal, state, and county correctional facilities into rehabilitation programs with daily involvement in educational, vocational, and rehabilitation programs;

(4) Eliminate required long mandated minimum sentences;

(5) Institute universal prerelease programs for all offenders with the goal of preparing them to transition into community-based addiction and mental health programs;

(6) Assuring that all released prisoners have access to publicly funded programs for addiction and mental health treatment upon release.

Endnotes

[i] Ditton, Paula M. Mental Health and Treatment of Inmates and Probationers, Bureau of Justice Statistics, July 11, 1999 (NCJ-174463), (http://www.ojp.usdoj.gov/bjs/)

[ii] American Psychiatric Association, Diagnostic and Statistical Manual of Mental Disorders (DSM IV), Fourth Edition, 1994 (Pgs. 424-429)

[iii] American Psychiatric Association, Diagnostic and Statistical Manual of Mental Disorders (DSM IV), Fourth Edition, 1994 (Pgs. 645-650)

[iv] Forrest, Gary G., Chemical Dependency and antisocial Personality Disorder Psychotherapy and Assessment Strategies, The Hawthorn Press, New York, April 1994

[v] Hempphill, James F.; Templeman, Ron; Wong, Stephen; and Hare,

Robert D. Psychopathy and Crime: Recidivism and Criminal Careers. IN: Cooke, David J.; Forth, Adelle E., and Hare, Robert D. ED: Psychopathy: Theory, Research, and implications for Society, Kluwar Academic Publishers, Boston, 1995

[vi] Grassian, Stuart, Psychopathological effects of solitary confinement, American Journal of Psychiatry, 140, 1450 - 1454 (1983)]

[vii] American Psychiatric Association, Diagnostic and Statistical Manual of Mental Disorders (DSM IV), Fourth Edition, 1994 (Pgs. 175-272)

[viii] Ditton, Paula M. Mental Health and Treatment of Inmates and Probationers, Bureau of Justice Statistics, July 11, 1999 (NCJ-174463), (http://www.ojp.usdoj.gov/bjs/)

[ix] Sabol, William, Urban Institute, Washington DC

[x] Abramsky, Sasha, When They Get Out, Atlantic Monthly, June, 1999 p. 30

Terrence Gorski of The Center for Applied Science (CENAPS) can be reached at: 17900 Dixie Hwy, Homewood, IL 60430, 708-799-5000; Fax: 708-799-5032, E-mail: info@enaps.com, Web: www.tgorski.com, www.cenaps.com, www.relapse.org. This article was originally published on the Addiction Website of Terence T. Gorski, www.tgorski.com , reprinted with permission.

The "Logical Illogic" of the Psycho-Logical

by Leon F. Seltzer Ph.D.

Part 1 Dreams

How does their very illogic make dreams the "royal road to the unconscious"?

Here's a dream reported by a client that vividly reveals the exquisitely logical connections between our waking concerns and nocturnal "hallucinations." The latter—paradoxically rational—narratives are crafted by our unconscious to illuminate, though symbolically, what we're still struggling to resolve inside our heads.

In my client's dream, he—Kevin (age 46)—is flagged down by a policeman for speeding. Although he's quite agitated by the situation, the officer himself displays an almost preternatural calm. Offhandedly, the cop mentions that his wife regularly voices apprehension that his excessive cell phone use could result in his developing a brain tumor. But he himself would never bother considering such a possibility. For he firmly believes it's best to live worry-free. Meanwhile, looking at the cop more closely, Kevin notices that his face is terribly damaged, decayed, dying—even though the cop seems blithely unaware of his appalling countenance.

So, what was the actual life situation that made this dream (baffling to my client, by the way) so "psychologically logical"?

Well, for the past several months Kevin had been having episodes of severe heart palpitations and an accelerated heart rate, causing him great anxiety. Obsessing about what negative things these scary symptoms might forebode—and whether their sheer intensity might eventually kill him—he was in a state of continuing, pronounced distress. Even though he had no history of heart problems, to rule out any serious physical condition, he'd seen several practitioners (holistic as well as traditional), been exhaustively

236

examined, and subject to as many diagnostic tests and procedures as his various practitioners could think of. Repeatedly, he was assured that his heart was fine. And though the alternative practitioners he consulted believed he was suffering from adrenal fatigue (which contributed to his physical complaints), he was told that his problems were essentially stress-related and psychological ...and altogether curable.

In short, the message Kevin received from all the professionals he'd sought help from was that his situation wasn't anywhere as serious as, subjectively, he experienced it. That is, "not to worry." And I, too, felt confident that once we worked through unresolved traumas from his past (which a series of present-day circumstances had re-vivified), his irksome symptoms would disappear. So among other things, I suggested that whenever he was suddenly beset by heart abnormalities, he simply reminds himself that they were a false alarm—a product (or by-product) of largely unconscious anxieties—rather than a forewarning of something catastrophic. And, overall, my various recommendations succeeded in calming him down considerably, as we proceeded to work on the likely psychological, and lifestyle, issues underlying his so-vexing physical problem. Still, inasmuch as his symptoms continued largely unabated, he couldn't entirely let go of his fears about how they might be significantly undermining his health.

Further, I explored with Kevin how his overblown fears and hypervigilance were making it almost impossible for him to relax (and insomnia was another one of his complaints). I also suggested how unconsciously he might be associating relaxation with increased vulnerability, so that if he should let his guard down something really awful could happen to him. And, of course, I instructed him to self-monitor (ahem, "police") his thoughts, so that if he found himself ruminating over worst case scenarios, he could employ the technique of "thought-stopping" and reassure himself that his symptoms weren't anywhere as serious as they appeared. While all this made sense to him, and he did receive some relief by actively contesting his irrational fears, at a deeper level he could hardly help but remain somewhat wary about his condition. Something at the very core of his psyche still felt compelled to worry.

So, if catastrophic thoughts of something terrible happening to him (something that none of the so-called "authorities" in his case could diagnose) continued to trouble his uneasy mind, how might these abiding concerns "logically" express themselves? Well, in his dream state. For that's the essential "work" of dreams: to remind us—dramatically and pictorially—of what, internally, doesn't yet feel resolved.

With all this in mind, let's return to Kevin's disturbing (and to him, "illogical") dream.

The dream begins with a policeman's pulling him over for speeding. His dangerous, or unsafe, driving can readily be seen as symbolizing his feelings about his coronary symptoms—in particular, his accelerated heart rate. The uniformed policeman (unmistakably emblematic of authority) can readily be linked to all the professionals he's seen, with no visible results to show for it. Besides representing the many different practitioners he's consulted, the officer would also appear to represent his not-entirely-successful efforts at "policing" his thoughts. After all, the cop is indirectly advising him to take things in stride and not worry, just as those in real-life authority have collectively instructed him.

Kevin's ambivalence about fully trusting the various "health police" who've intervened to assist him is pointedly suggested by the fact that the cop in his dream has something seriously wrong with him, as revealed by his corroded, disintegrating visage. So my client's subterranean doubts about whether it's really safe to be reassuring himself is "logically" supported by the officer's actual appearance, which sharply contradicts the personal philosophy he's so eager to impart to him. The cop's message about not letting anything upset him loses all authority because he himself is in mortal danger yet utterly oblivious to it. And—because dreams are frequently multidimensional, with people and circumstances frequently carrying more than a single meaning—the cop's compromised appearance can also be viewed as reflecting how my client unconsciously (and fearfully) views himself. So, under these circumstances, training himself not to worry might really set him up for an "unseemly" demise. (Death by oversight, if you will.)

Literally, of course—or rather, out of context—Kevin's dream would appear extraneous to everything he was going through, not logical at all. But figuratively it renders, as logically as any simple "fiction" could, the precise dimensions of his "two minds" about his condition. His unconscious nocturnal imaginings give creative voice to all the doubts and confusions he's endeavored to "edit out" in his waking hours. His dream is as compact, as laden with meaning, as the most eloquent lyric poem. The cop may have the authority to give him a ticket (as do all the practitioners charging him for their "authoritative" advice). Still, how much of this authority ought he to respect when the cop/authority of his dream can't even notice his own symptoms, so horrifically blatant to my client. Though, presumably, his cell phone has already done grave harm to him, he nonetheless glibly preaches the doctrine of "all is well."

Clearly, this is the issue my client felt compelled—however unconsciously—to work on (and why, from Jung to the present day, therapists can talk about our nighttime visions as "dream work"). He desperately wanted to believe the positive things all his "experts" (myself included) were telling him. Yet he remained symptomatic. Just as the happy-go-lucky officer's face really was injured, periodically his heart—despite all the reassurances he'd received—just couldn't seem to beat right. And even when he felt calm, beyond a certain point this relaxed state could itself trigger another anxiety attack. Professional opinion notwithstanding, who knows?

Maybe it was dangerous to let his guard down.

Kevin's dream was revelatory. Unquestionably, it betrayed the unresolved doubts about his condition that, consciously at least, he thought he'd conquered. Given the particularly disturbing nature of his symptoms, however, it made complete sense—that is, was subjectively logical—that he couldn't help but be afflicted by some remnants of suspicion.

Finally, it may be that the innermost operations of the human psyche are most accurately deciphered through analyzing our nighttime fantasies. However irrational they may seem to our waking mind, they embody their own profound logic. And although such "trans-rational" logic may frequently be at odds with what—objectively, at least—would appear logical, psychologically their inherent reasoning is impeccable.

Part 2. The Paradoxical Rationale for Self-Sabotage

There's a "logical illogic" in the psycho-logical. Do you seem to struggle in life much more than others? Do your efforts to succeed regularly get derailed? Is following through on your plans (well-conceived as they may be) typically problematic? Do you do stupid or impulsive things when you know better? Do your relationships start out promising, but usually go south—as though somehow you just can't help saying or doing something to capsize them? Are you perhaps a lot better at making money than holding onto it?

If any of these descriptions rings true for you, you may be guilty of self-sabotage. If you're disciplined enough to work hard at accomplishing a goal, yet routinely do something rash or imprudent to undermine it, your behavior may actually be more motivated than you imagine. In Part 1 of this post I talked about the psychology—or rather, "logical illogic"—of dreams. In this part (as well as the three to follow) I'll focus on the curiously inverted rationality of self sabotaging/self-defeatist behaviors. So if you resonate with some of the above characterizations, it's probably not a coincidence. Author of your own life script, you may have—however unconsciously—been "planning" your own failures all along.

Sound illogical? Well, the mind has its own logic. And it's frequently at odds with what, objectively, would appear reasonable. Most defense mechanisms, for example, are counterproductive. Yet they do serve the immediate psychological function of protecting you from possibly overwhelming feelings of anxiety, guilt, or shame. Regardless of the ultimately negative repercussions of, say, regression, repression, or denial, such self-protective mechanisms do alleviate what otherwise might overpower your coping resources.

Take, for instance, your key relationship. It may not make much sense to lose your temper and turn on the person you're most committed to. But it's psychologically understandable (i.e., "logical") that in an emotionally dependent relationship, your anger might help mitigate the feelings of vulnerability such dependency is apt to evoke. If you actually dared admit to the other person how much you needed their caring, closeness, and support—and, alas, they refused you-you'd wind up experiencing the sharp sting of rejection and abandonment: two of the most distressful emotions we humans are susceptible to.

It's only reasonable, therefore, that in your attempts to avoid such hurt or humiliation, when you begin to doubt the other's commitment to you, you might berate them—and thereby "succeed" in nullifying the perceived threat they embody. Practically, you're abandoning them to preclude the possibility of feeling abandoned by them. They can't "fire" you, for in the moment you've—preemptively—fired them.

In short, on one level it's illogical that you'd verbally attack the person you're most devoted to. But on another, it's altogether logical that you might get angry to increase your emotional distance when their behavior (however subliminally) suggests their ability to hurt you. Not willing to risk feeling rebuffed by their possible disinterest, unconcern, or disapproval, you're likely to criticize or otherwise "invalidate" them. (And in this regard, see my earlier post, "What Your Anger May Be Hiding.") We humans have the potential to do almost anything—and to employ whatever defenses may be at our disposal—to re-secure at least part of our emotional equilibrium when it's experienced as in jeopardy.

As opposed to logic, "psycho-logic" follows its own set of rules. And these rules can be quite as subjective (and idiosyncratic) as they are paradoxical. To the psyche, winning can feel like losing. And success like failure—and, perhaps even more perversely, failure like success. Although it would hardly make sense to an observer, if failing at something enables you to avoid a situation linked to intolerable fear, panic, or shame, then it does—at least immediately—allow you to emerge triumphant. Even as you experience disappointment, you may breathe a welcome sigh of relief.

By now, just about everyone is familiar with the ironic concept, fear of success. And if failure is able, "successfully," to alleviate that fear, then it's only logical—or psycho-logically reasonable-that we might actually choose to fail.

Part 3. The "Programming" of Self-Sabotage

What's the "logical illogic" behind self-defeat? The Key Determinant of Self-Sabotaging Behavior

Most everything that's psychologically dysfunctional has its origins in outdated childhood programs. These are programs keyed to your child self's perception of how best to adjust to irrational family requirements or demands. I call these adaptations "survival programs," for in growing up it generally feels crucial to do all that's possible to form a secure bond with your parents. After all, regardless of how inept they may have been as caretakers, how could you possibly have survived without them? Whether you were abused or neglected, they were still the only ones that could supply you with food and shelter when you were without the resources to provide them yourself.

Unfortunately, these programs of adaptation, more or less useful as a child, typically become ever less so as you age. And now, probably as unconscious as they are entrenched, these programs may be very hard to recognize—which is absolutely pivotal if you're successfully to confront, and revise, them.

Take, for example, a client I once saw that simply wasn't able to ask for what she wanted. Her passivity caused her endless frustrations—both at work and at home. Before she could overcome her enormous barriers about asserting herself, she first needed to become aware of just where such self-sabotaging/self-defeating behavior originated. And what I helped her recognize was that, as a child, directly requesting what she desired was—parentally speaking-unacceptable.

The message she regularly received when, initially, she approached her parents with her wants and needs was that she was selfish, that she only thought of herself. And when, "adaptively," she began to subordinate her needs to others', her parents showed more approval of her. Logically enough, she concluded that if she were to feel safely attached to her (conditionally accepting) parents, she either had to suppress the expression of her needs or repress them altogether.

It was only when her adult self was able to get into communication with her anxious, insecure child self (the highly influential fragment of her being which still governed her behavior) that this non-nurturing "survival" program could be re-written. But, again, not until she was able to convince her doubting inner child that this self-deprived—and self-depriving—period of her life was forever over . . . and that it was now safe, even essential, for her to explicitly make her wants and needs known to others. Only then could she liberate herself from this antiquated program of self-denial. And, as is typical in such cases, this "relinquishing-the-past" process wasn't all that easy for her. For altering deeply embedded behaviors that have become fused with one's very way of being requires nothing less than a fundamental alteration in one's core sense of self.

Internal conflicts about change are definitely resolvable. But generally it's a gradual process, and involves overcoming deep-seated resistances. Just consider, for instance, how many times you've heard someone say: "That's just who I am," or "That's the way I'm made," or "I've always been this way." It's typical to assume that your habits reflect who you are rather than how you've programmed yourself to adapt to family-of-origin imperatives. Which is perhaps the main reason that you need to grasp the external forces originally contributing to your current-day dysfunctions before you can—deliberately—set about changing them.

Modifying your behavior—or better, reclaiming the behavior you once experienced an urgent need to disown—is inevitably laden with negative expectations. So again, it's "only logical" that however maladaptive that behavior might have become, striving to alter it may feel gravely threatening to your fundamental belief system. But if you're committed to change, eventually you'll succeed. For a while though, your scared or hesitant child part may well protest your adult self's commitment to "correct" the past.

So don't be surprised if, self-protectively, the child residing within you engenders symptoms of anxiety, physiologically pleading with you to avoid carrying out unprecedented behaviors it experiences as mortally threatening to its welfare. Reprogramming old survival tapes may require you to attend, and sympathetically listen, to that "scaredy-cat" part of yourself—even as you seek to reassure that frightened, much younger self. Still, as long as you're committed to change, and refuse to be controlled by outdated programming, you'll eventually triumph over it.

Other Sources of Self-Sabotaging Behavior

Before listing the kinds of core negative beliefs that fuel self-sabotage, I should probably add that such defeating behaviors derive from more than childhood circumstances (including relationships not just with family, but also with peers, relatives, and other authority figures). There are at least three additional sources for self-sabotaging programs.

For one thing, self-defeating patterns can derive from anything you experience as traumatic-experience, that is, as a grave threat to your survival (or at least the survival of your ego). Virtually by definition, trauma "sensitizes" you, or makes you overreact to, any stimuli perceived as sufficiently similar to what's become linked to the event that earlier alarmed or shocked you. Yet because in such instances your reaction is likely to be, say, overly avoidant or aggressive, such exaggerated behavior will frequently end up defeating you. Self-protectively necessary as, inside, it may feel to you, in the present it's distorted, ill-advised.

For example, if you're a veteran afflicted with PTSD, it's understandable that you might dart beneath a desk every time you hear a plane flying overhead. But in the here-and-now it still doesn't make any rational sense. In fact, it might be said that trauma leads to "extreme logic"—a logic that's become absolute and no longer hinges on any particular situation to justify it.

Another cause of self-sabotaging behavior relates to substances, relationships, or activities that in the past have reduced stress or anxiety levels. Most addictions (from chain smoking to excessive drinking, gambling, shopping, or sexing) serve this important function. So it's only reasonable that you could get caught up in behavior that, while in the moment it alleviates distress, also makes it impossible for you to achieve what it is you really want. In fact, any strategy you've come to rely on almost exclusively to reduce stress can wind up being self-defeating.

Lastly, there are certain personality traits that if not overcome (or at least mitigated) can promote self-sabotage. For instance, if you were born shy you probably tried to escape unfamiliar social situations. Timorous by nature, they just felt too scary to you. But unless you eventually prevailed over this innate reticence, you'd end up socially phobic. Controlled by fears of "exposure" (tied to ancient feelings of intolerable vulnerability), you'd remain—well—socially retarded, behind the curve in developing interpersonal skills and confidence. And your passivity and pronounced tendency to avoid new encounters would almost guarantee that, both personally and professionally, you'd never reach your full potential.

Core Negative Beliefs That Foster Self-Sabotage

From a difficult childhood environment to dysfunctional conditioning resulting from unresolved trauma—and from maladaptive behaviors to relieve stress, to factors in one's native constitution or temperament—we've looked at different ways people get programmed to sabotage themselves. Now it's time to pinpoint some of the most common categories of self-beliefs (typically below conscious awareness) that give rise to such self-defeating behaviors.

Within each category, I've listed several specific self-statements that, if reflective of your underlying belief system, may well be preventing you from successfully completing (or even undertaking) what otherwise might be quite possible for you. Another way of saying this is that if, deep down, you feel you can't accomplish something, you really won't let yourself try—or try hard enough—to succeed.

Moreover, imminent success can tap into abhorrent memories of past punishment. As an example, let's say that as a child your father couldn't handle your doing any better, whether academically or at sports, than he himself did when he was younger. And so he regularly found something (anything!) to attack you for every time you performed exceptionally. Time after time he—well—sabotaged your success by finding a way to make you pay an exceedingly high price for it. Given such a scenario, doesn't it make perfect, "logical" sense that you'd end up with mixed feelings about succeeding? That you might hold yourself back from achieving what's well within your reach? That, unconsciously, you'd be motivated to sabotage yourself?

Sure, your behavior could be considered self-defeating. Yet it's logically connected to the emotional uneasiness that may in the past have become inextricably bound to the very thought of superiority or success. In the present day, the underlying programming that continues to "compel" your behavior may be flagrantly irrational. But that wasn't the case originally, when you couldn't help but link succeeding to all sorts of negative consequences.

Obviously, the logic of the past can become the illogic of the present. The problem is that outdated modes of reasoning can still feel logical to you and thereby dictate your behavior—even when the circumstances of your life have changed dramatically. And if you've gained little to no insight on how, willfully, you may have been "contriving" your own failures, you may go on rationalizing them ad infinitum. Meanwhile, through sheer force of habit, the "practice" of self sabotage may have become more and more deeply ingrained in you. The end result of such unfortunate self-conditioning is that unless you're able to discover the true source of your dysfunctional behavior—and, additionally, convince that much younger part of self that it's no longer required or makes any sense—you'll never be able to fully outgrow it.

And to the degree you remain oblivious to the dynamics of such behavior, it will continue to control you. . ... As in, meet your own worst enemy.

Part 4 Self-Sabotage and Your "Outer Child" (

As illogical as it might seem, your child self may be your saboteur.

Your inner child, or child within, is a popular term in the so-called "recovery field" (recovery, that is, from having grown up in a dysfunctional family). This catch-all phrase typically refers to that wounded part of you that got left behind—the neglected or abused fragment of self that, though you may not hear its muffled voice, still calls out for recognition, understanding, and support. In a word, for the nurturing it never received. It's scared and lonely, and it feels weak, vulnerable, and abandoned.

But how about what, unconventionally, might be referred to as your outer child, or child without? These are designations meant to describe the segment of self that in the here-and-now can "act out"—rashly and illogically—past needs and desires. Or powerful feelings that earlier never could be expressed (not to mention, resolved). In fact, all "acting out" behaviors are contrived to reduce current-day tensions or anxieties through giving unmonitored vent to thoughts, feelings, wants, and needs.

Unfortunately, however, such a potentially healthy release is at the questionable discretion of your outer child. And this is the impulsive, careless, uncensored part of you that's apt to express itself with little or no regard for possible consequences. So when your outer child heedlessly manifests itself, it can do so in ways that get you into all sorts of trouble, and engender a variety of thorny problems. Problems that serve only to make matters worse and increase your frustrations. After all, it's the most undiscriminating, undisciplined part of you: unruly, demanding, self-indulgent, and unrestrained.

Under its rebellious influence, you're at serious risk of giving in to immediately gratifying addictions; going into mindless rages (possibly directed toward those you care about most); delaying—and even abandoning—projects that require your self-discipline and perseverance; and so on, and so on. At such times, your impetuous child part literally takes over your adult self and acts on its own volition, pre-empting or overriding how you, the adult, would prefer to behave.

Even when you know very well what's in your best interests, if you remain oblivious to this outer child it can emerge out of nowhere and become your saboteur, willfully submerging your interests to its own.

Earlier, I published a two-part post entitled, "Feeling Good—Vs. Feeling Good About Ourselves," which suggested that when we act, self-indulgently, to feel better in the moment, ultimately we feel not better but worse about ourselves. And the problem with unwittingly allowing your outer child to triumph over your better judgment is that for the sake of immediate gratification you'll end up sacrificing what's actually much more satisfying and meaningful to you.

Needless to say, it's crucial that your child—or emotional—self be governed (though not squelched) by your more rational adult self. For when feelings and impulses are permitted to play the lead role in your life drama, you risk making decisions that are poorly considered—or hardly considered at all. And such imprudence is likely to compromise your welfare, undermine your key relationships, and eventually compromise your self-regard. Your "inner child" needs to be heard and attended to—and this is actually what self-nurturing is all about (see, incidentally, an older post of mine on this topic). On the contrary, however, your "outer child" needs to be regulated, controlled, and subdued. For as already suggested, permitting your impulses free reign is apt to lead to repercussions you're likely to regret later. Repercussions that in your acting (or reacting) too hastily, you simply couldn't recognize—much less evaluate.

This is why when you feel really strongly about something, it's wise to step back and ask yourself whether you can afford to act on this feeling. It's likely that you've just gotten a button pushed, or let your imagination run away with you. Or that you're feeling distraught-inordinately angry, frightened, or depressed. These are all emotional states in which your better, more logical judgment may no longer be available, so that you need to do everything in your power to restore equilibrium. Whether you arrange a spontaneous session of yoga or Qigong, jog around the block, or undertake a session of self-hypnosis, meditation, visualization or guided imagery, it's essential that you succeed in quieting down your emotions. Remember, the emotional reasoning of the child may masquerade as rational, but from an adult perspective it's anything but.

Different (Though Complementary) Vantage Points on Self-Sabotage

Various authors have written on the controversial subject of self-defeating behaviors. And many of them specifically allude to their emanating from the childish, impulsive part of ourselves—that part unable, or unwilling, to see beyond the present moment. As I've repeatedly stressed, the logic of the child (i.e., the "logic" of immediate gratification—or, "If it feels good, do it!") becomes the illogic of the adult. Here, I've room to discuss only three of these writings.

However, my highly selective coverage should be suggestive.

Your Own Worst Enemy: Understanding the Paradox of Self-Defeating Behavior (1993) by Steven Berglas and Roy F. Baumeister argues that there are multiple explanations for why individuals sabotage themselves. These accounts range from miscalculating future risks, to irrational feelings of invincibility, to choking under pressure, to self-handicapping, to overly costly (or Pyrrhic) revenge. Typically, such individuals are not out to destroy themselves but rather trying to:

- save themselves from successes they fear they can't sustain (cf. the negative belief from childhood, "I will fail," mentioned in Part 3);
- prevent public humiliation (cf. from that same list, "I'm contemptible");
- rectify childhood wrongs; or simply
- maximize pleasure—though in unheeding, or otherwise misguided, ways.

Examples that Berglas and Baumeister provide include: battered women who regularly return to their abusive partners; athletes, whose bodies are absolutely essential to their success, abusing them with drugs and alcohol; entrepreneurs who take illogical—and ruinous—risks when they've already secured their fortune; and politicians and evangelists who engage in scandalous behaviors virtually guaranteeing their downfall. Not to mention, of course, we more common folk who (quite aware of the dangers) drive without seat belts, indulge in extramarital affairs, and—counter to doctor's orders—eat sugary sweets that exacerbate our issues with cholesterol.

After beginning work on this post, I discovered the work of psychotherapist, Susan Anderson-more specifically, her book, *Taming Your Outer Child: A Revolutionary Program to Overcome Self-Defeating Patterns* (2011). Much earlier, I'd typed into Google the phrase "child without" (vs. "child within") and received no citations, tentatively leading me to conclude that my designation was as novel as I'd hoped. But when, much more recently, I re-googled the topic-this time employing the alternate title, "outer child"— I was immediately directed to Anderson's groundbreaking work, which had in fact been evolving for over a decade. (So much, then, for my originality!)

Though developed at far greater length, Anderson's views are extremely similar to my own. The quoted material below should suggest some of her key ideas:

- "Outer child is an overarching concept [of self-sabotage] that encompasses defense mechanisms, character traits, knee-jerk reactions, habits and compulsions—all of your maladaptive behavior patterns.
- Whereas Inner child is all about feelings, Outer child is all about behavior.
- Outer child is the selfish, obstinate, impulsive, self-centered part of all of us."
- Outer wants what Outer wants NOW and overrules you, the adult, in getting it.
- Outer Child is the hidden "Chuckie" of the personality. Even the nicest people we know can act like an eight-year old with a full blown conduct disorder (perhaps not in public) when they feel rejected, dismissed, abandoned.
- Outer child is born of unresolved abandonment. It wreaks havoc in your relationships when it acts out your inner child's primal fear of abandonment.
- When your adult self and your inner child are out of alignment, Outer child gains power and acts out your neglected needs and feelings however it wants—to hell with your goals. Bottom line: If your head and heart remain disconnected, you can expect Outer Child to become more and more emboldened to butt into your life.
- The antidote is to create a deeper [and more loving] internal bond [i.e., between your inner child and adult]."

On her Outer Child website, Anderson presents an Outer Child Checklist with no fewer than 60 items to help you determine how many such traits you (and/or those close to you) may embody. And the author emphasizes that all of them reflect the "illogical thinking" of the outer child (though I'd call it "logically illogical" in that so many of these behaviors are contrived—

rationally enough—by the child to protect its fragile ego). I've chosen just a few of these negative characteristics to demonstrate how blatantly irrational—at least from a longer term, adult perspective—these tendencies can be:

- "Outer Child doesn't like to do things that are good for you. Outer would rather do something that will make you fat, broke, or pregnant.
- Outer Child loves to feed its emotional hunger with things like shopping, sex, sugar that only makes you hungrier in the end.
- Outer projects its faults on your mate. Likewise onto your children.
- Outer Child enjoys playing the victim, that is, when not playing the martyr.
- Outer Child has a chip on its shoulder, which it disguises as assertiveness. . . . [It] develops a 'tude' to keep people at bay. It's trying to protect your inner child's feelings of loneliness and vulnerability [and, yet again, here is the self-defensive logic of the child].
- Outer Child is highly principled: it scrupulously obeys the pleasure principle [!]."

Overall, the unflattering portrait that emerges from Anderson's varied descriptions are of that part of you who thinks and speaks in absolutes; won't take responsibility for its behaviors; reacts defensively; is impatient, impulsive, self-indulgent, and self-righteous; is oblivious to (or even reckless about) the consequences of its actions; and is unwilling to respect the rights—or accommodate the viewpoints—of others. Ultimately, it can be seen as the arch enemy of you-your essential, more grown-up self, which includes your goals, ideals, and aspirations. Indeed, the very heart and soul of you (vs., that is, your unruly, egocentric, even "brattish," self).

And speaking of "brattish," the final book on one's outer child that I'll mention is by Pauline Wallin and actually goes by the title, *Self-defeating* (2004). Similar to Anderson, Wallin explores the early childhood roots of this so-called brattish self. But she also looks at the social and cultural conditions in the U.S. that provide the breeding grounds for such reprehensible self-centeredness, willfulness, and feelings of entitlement. Having its own emphasis, yet overlapping with Anderson's thesis and characterizations, this work unfavorably views your "inner brat" as pouting, sulking, antagonistic, ill-tempered, and blaming others whenever it's not getting its way.

Finally, it's really the childishly self-absorbed, narcissistic proclivities in all of us that compel this selfish behavior—which in turn leads to our self-defeat. Rather less sympathetic to these unfortunate childhood remnants than is Anderson, Wallin focuses on such dishonorable internal forces as basically constituting a "spoiled child," demanding that its needs and desires be immediately attended to—with no consideration of whether the person attending to them might be inconvenienced, hurt, or damaged in the process.

Whether you prefer to see this aspect of yourself as your "outer child" or "inner brat," Wallin and Anderson both go to substantial lengths in describing how best to "tame" it. I'd therefore recommend that anyone who relates only too easily to their many characterizations take the opportunity to investigate their work further.

Part 5. Self-Sabotage as Passive Aggression Toward the Self

Could you be—unawares—a mental and emotional masochist?

In self-sabotage you "act out" internal conflicts by first moving toward a goal—then retreating from it. "I can do it" is offset by "I can't do it." "I want it" is overridden by "No, I don't want it." "I deserve it" countermanded by "I don't deserve it." The net result of such an ambivalent—or negative—attitude toward yourself is hardly to be envied. For the outcome is either immobilization (at times, an existential paralysis so exquisitely sculpted that push is perfectly balanced with pull, and pull with push). Or you're impelled—or rather, unconsciously compelled-to do everything in your power to defeat yourself.

From deep within, as a kind of hapless puppet, you may be controlled by programs so antagonistic or contradictory that it's simply impossible to achieve what, otherwise, might be well within your grasp. And insufficiently aware of the adverse self-beliefs underlying such programming—beliefs most likely derived from negative messages you regularly received from your parents—you can't confront (let alone resolve) your deepest conflicts. As I like to put it, until you've assimilated your past (i.e., fully "digested" it), it will keep repeating on you.

Needless to say, as long as you remain mostly unconscious about how self-defeatingly you've interpreted what happened to you in the past, you really can't allow yourself to straightforwardly follow your dreams. Unaware of the sabotaging aspects of your personality—those earlier self denigrating parts afflicted with feelings of futility, incompetence, or unworthiness—you'll habitually trip yourself up.

Your own very worst enemy, you'll castigate yourself for shortcomings, experience guilt and shame for sins never committed, and routinely snatch defeat from the jaws of victory. Moreover, you may (self-debasingly) permit others to take what, unconsciously, you feel unworthy to accept yourself—whether that be recognition for some accomplishment you were chiefly responsible for, or a promotion that by rights should have been yours.

Passive aggression toward the self is fundamentally about self-punishment. After all, if you're self-disapproving, don't much like yourself, and have never been able to fully embrace yourself (flaws and all), your ultimately counterproductive behavior will reflect this negative self-regard. It's as though you've given—let's say—your overly judgmental parents permanent residency inside your head (and rent free, at that!), with the inevitable result that these perennial authority figures constantly remind you that you're not good enough, that you can't live up to their expectations.

Sadly, in the recesses of your brain, their critical voice has become your own. This unfortunate "importation" phenomenon is what psychoanalysts commonly call "introjects"—wherein you've unconsciously imbibed the detrimental messages about self that your once terribly significant others (however inadvertently) imparted to you

Now, if you actively aggress against yourself, you're probably aware of it. You'd have tremendous difficulty denying it—such as pretending you didn't just punch yourself in the gut. Or cut off your eyebrows. Or in some other way disfigure yourself (and in this respect consider individuals—particularly adolescents—who harm, injure, or mutilate themselves). To give a few additional examples of active self-aggression, might it be that you curse yourself each time you make a mistake? Or secretly root for your opponent to defeat you? Or—to really take it to the extreme—set fire to something you love (and without any motive to collect on your insurance policy either!)?

But, counter to active self-aggression, if you passively aggress against yourself, you could deny it indefinitely. Rationalize or makes excuses for it, blame it on someone else, remain totally oblivious to it, and so on. Which is all too easy to do when you don't have much of an idea about what—unconsciously—motivated you to defeat yourself in the first place. Still, if you're to appreciate why things may frequently turn out badly for you, it could be extremely useful to evaluate your behavior in terms of passive-aggression toward the self (a phrase I've yet to see employed either in the literature on passive-aggression or self-sabotage).

Further, it might be worthwhile to consider some key characteristics of passive-aggressive behavior as they're delineated in the mental health practitioner's diagnostic bible, DSM-IV. In this comprehensive manual of mental disorders, Passive-Aggressive Personality Disorder—which is also referred to as Negativistic Personality Disorder—is characterized primarily as "passive resistance to demands for adequate performance in social and occupational situations." Although this description clearly implies an interpersonal context for such behavior, in the case of passive aggression directed toward one's own self, the resistance isn't from without but within.

The battle is far less with others than between the adult part of you (which, being your rational self, would like to be effective and succeed) and the child part of you (which has its own—ahem-"logically illogical" reasons for methodically undermining your efforts). Once again, this is the immature, "acting out" part of you whose motives can be understood either as impulsive (i.e., acting solely for immediate gratification) or reactive (i.e., negatively—and hyper-sensitively-responding to the memory of circumstances that occurred many years, or even decades, ago).

Additional characterizations in DSM-IV for the Passive-Aggressive Personality Disorder can similarly be adapted to depict passive-aggression in its inward (as opposed to outward) form. You may want to mull over the various features of this disorder as you also reflect upon how each description might be modified—or re-perceived—to coalesce with this post's portrayal of self-aggression. And actually, the wording in some of these depictions can be viewed as already blending in with what's been described here (i.e., may hardly require any semantic adjustments at all). Here are, according to DSM-IV, some other facets of the disorder.

The passive-aggressive individual:

- Complains of being misunderstood and unappreciated by others;
- May be sullen, irritable, impatient, argumentative, cynical, skeptical, and contrary;
- Unreasonably criticizes and scorns authority;
- Expresses envy and resentment toward those apparently more fortunate;
- Voices exaggerated and persistent complaints of personal misfortune;
- Alternates between hostile defiance and contrition [implied here, of course, is rebelliousness toward others—but such individuals, or groups, may actually be "stand-ins" for the introjects so firmly ensconced in your own head];
- Expresses opposition through procrastinating, forgetting, stubbornness, and intentional inefficiency—especially in reaction to tasks assigned by authority figures [again, compare this portrayal to negative reactions to the introject "authorities" occupying space in your brain); and
- Holds a negative view toward the future.

To conclude, if you see yourself—to whatever degree—as having committed self-sabotage in the past, and feel that you're vulnerable to further self-defeating behaviors in the future, it only makes sense to identify just what in your background may still be calling out for resolution. Although, admittedly, this is an oversimplification and won't apply to everything that may now be obstructing your path forward, you might wish to consider that (as Werner Erhard, founder of EST, once said) until you've "completed" your relationship with your parents, all your relationships will be about your parents.

So it may well behoove you to do some sort of life retrospective and explore what from your past (whether or not it relates specifically to your caretakers) may still require "processing through" …if, that is, you're to live fully in the present, unimpeded by old, still "psycho-active" programs that continue to hinder your rightful pursuit of happiness.

Originally published in Psychology Today *11/16/10, reprinted with permission.*

Mourning and Grieving

by Ben Colodzin Ph.D.

Many events in life, such as the loss of loved ones, may evoke grief. Our culture has not been particularly encouraging in allowing the expression of grief, especially among men, who are often taught it 'isn't manly' to feel or express this type of emotion. We need to overcome this resistance and learn how to do it. As the psychiatrist Elizabeth Kubler-Ross noted in her landmark work with people with terminal illnesses, people go through various stages in coming to accept overwhelming traumatic events such as an impending terminal illness. She identified the stages as 1) denial (it isn't happening); 2) bargaining (it's happening a little bit, but not really serious); 3) anger (I am so mad that it's happening; 4) grieving (I am so deeply sad that it's happening); and finally 5) acceptance (I accept that it' is happening).

People can experience the feelings associated with these various stages with many different types of traumatic events, and can get 'stuck' at any stage. The stage of moving through mourning and grieving of what has been lost is generally considered to be important to the healing process and in coming to a place of acceptance of whatever has happened in one's life. One size definitely does not fit all, and mourning and grieving can occur in near-infinite ways.

In some of our group meetings at CTF, we have called upon outside-the-box resources to help people understand the importance of mourning and grieving whatever painful losses they have experienced that have not yet been grieved. To this end, we have shared with each group for the past five years an audio lecture by a Native American teacher named Martin Prechtel who was trained by Mayan medicine people in Guatemala. Although we cannot reproduce that lecture here in a book, it has consistently produced profound effects for a large number of the men who listened to it. It helped many understand the need for grieving, and to begin to invite the grief locked up in their hearts to be acknowledged. While almost everyone reported this was a difficult journey, they also reported that burdens were lifted and new insights were achieved.

And so we want to acknowledge the value of this inspiring talk here. The lecture is on a CD titled *Grief And Praise* and it is available for purchase by the speaker, and is also posted on the internet as a YouTube audio lecture (on YouTube search, enter 'Martin Prechtel Grief and Praise'). In it, Mr. Prechtel describes a Native American view of grieving as not merely necessary, but as a sacred act. He describes grief and praise as two sides of the same coin, both living in one's heart. It is a very convincing discussion that helps people who have been avoiding the pain of feeling their grief to realize that doing so, although it may be very difficult in the short term, is actually of great importance to their health and spiritual development.

If you have the ability to get a copy of that CD into your prison, we can recommend it as one way we have used successfully to touch upon this emotionally-charged subject in a way that illuminates its sacred quality. If not accessible, please use whatever you can find that encourages you to respect the grief that may exist in your own heart, and to give it a chance to speak to you. It is a natural human emotion that may have gotten frozen into numbness in anyone who has experienced severe traumas. As Mr. Prechtel noted in his most recent book:

> "Grief expressed out loud for someone we have lost, or a country or home we have lost, is in itself the greatest praise we could ever give them. Grief is praise, because it is the natural way love honors what it misses."
>
> —Martin Prechtel[1]

---

[1] From *The Smell of Rain on Dust: Grief and Praise.* (Doc Piper commented that Chapter Eight of this book—Too Big, Too Sour, Too Hard, Too Old: The Black Hole of Ungrieved War—was the best thing he had ever seen written on the consequences of war. He said he wished he had written it).

The Wounded Healer

by Paul Levy

The wounded healer refers psychologically to the capacity "to be at home in the darkness of suffering and there to find germs of light and recovery with which, as though by enchantment, to bring forth Asclepius, the sun-like healer." The archetype of the wounded healer reveals to us that it is only by being willing to face, consciously experience and go through our wound do we receive its blessing. To go through our wound is to embrace, assent, and say "yes" to the mysteriously painful new place in ourselves where the wound is leading us. Going through our wound, we can allow ourselves to be re-created by the wound.

Our wound is not a static entity, but rather a continually unfolding dynamic process that manifests, reveals and incarnates itself through us, which is to say that our wound is teaching us something about ourselves. Going through our wound means realizing we will never again be the same when we get to the other side of this initiatory process. Going through our wound is a genuine death experience, as our old self "dies" in the process, while a new, more expansive and empowered part of ourselves is potentially born. Going through and embracing our wound as a part of ourselves is radically different than circumnavigating and going around (avoiding), or getting stuck in and endlessly, obsessively recreating (being taken over by) our wound. The event of our wounding is simultaneously catalyzing a deeper (potential) healing process which requires our active engagement, thus "wedding" us to a deeper level of our being. Jung's closest colleague, Marie Louise Von Franz, said "the wounded healer IS the archetype of the Self [our wholeness, the God within] and is at the bottom of all genuine healing procedures."

The Wounded Healer *by Paul Levy was originally published at www.awakeninthedream.com. This excerpt is reprinted with permission.*

Kindness

by Naomi Shihab Nye

Before you know what kindness really is, you must lose things,
Feel the future dissolve in a moment, like salt in a weakened broth.
What you held in your hand, what you counted and carefully saved,
All this must go,
So you know how desolate the landscape can be, between the regions of
kindness.
How you ride and ride, thinking the bus will never stop, the passengers eating
maize and chicken
Will stare out the window forever.

Before you learn the tender gravity of kindness
You must travel to where the Indian in a white poncho lies dead by the side
of the road.
You must see how this could be you,
How he too was someone who journeyed through the night with plans
And the simple breath that kept him alive.

Before you know kindness as the deepest thing inside,
You must know sorrow as the other deepest thing.
You must wake up with sorrow,
You must speak to it till your voice catches the thread of all sorrows,
And you see the size of the cloth.

Then it is only kindness that makes sense anymore,
Only kindness that ties your shoes

And sends you into the day to mail letters and purchase bread,
Only kindness that raises its head from the crowd of the world to say
It is I you have been looking for,
And then goes with you everywhere,
Like a shadow or a friend.

From Words Under the Words *by Naomi S. Nye. 1980., Reprinted with permission.*

Afterword

From all of us who have contributed to this work, we end this collection with the motto and the ethic that inspired us and offer it once again to you:

HELPING OURSELVES BY HELPING OTHERS

Thanks, Ed. Thanks, Doc. We're proud of what you did.

www.ingramcontent.com/pod-product-compliance
Lightning Source LLC
LaVergne TN
LVHW041152080426
835511LV00006B/564